ROTTEN ROMANS

Terry Deary

Illustrated by **Martin Brown**

SCHOLASTIC

With thanks to Helen for her research.
Sine qua non

Scholastic Children's Books,
Euston House, 24 Eversholt Street,
London NW1 1DB, UK

A division of Scholastic Ltd
London ~ New York ~ Toronto ~ Sydney ~ Auckland
Mexico City ~ New Delhi ~ Hong Kong

First published in the UK by Scholastic Ltd, 1994
Some of the material in this book has previously been published in *Horrible Histories The Awesome Ancient Quiz Book*
This abridged edition published by Scholastic Ltd, 2013

Text copyright © Terry Deary, 1994, 2001, 2013
Illustrations copyright © Martin Brown, 1994, 2001, 2013
Index by Caroline Hamilton

ISBN 978 1407 13577 9

Printed and bound by CPI Group (UK) Ltd, Croydon, CR0 4YY

2 4 6 8 10 9 7 5 3 1

The right of Terry Deary and Martin Brown to be identified as the author and illustrator of this work respectively has been asserted by them in accordance with the Copyright, Designs and Patents Act, 1988.

Contents

EEEEK!

Introduction

History can be horrible. Horribly hard to learn. The trouble is it keeps on changing. In maths, two and two is usually four – and in science water is always made up of hydrogen and oxygen.

But in history things aren't that simple. In history a "fact" is sometimes not a fact at all. Really it's just someone's "opinion". And opinions can be different for different people.

For example ... you probably think your teacher is more horrible than the cold cabbage and custard you had for school dinner. That's your opinion. But teacher's mum probably thinks he's sweeter than tea with six sugars. That's her opinion.

You could both be right – or both be wrong...

See what I mean? Both right, both wrong!

Of course, honest answers like these don't get you gold stars. No! Teachers will try to tell you there are "right" and "wrong" answers even if there aren't.

There are worse things than horrible history. Want to know what? Teachers' jokes are more horrible than the **Tower of London Torture Chamber...**

So, history can be horrible. But when you find the real truth about the past you can suddenly discover it's **horribly fascinating**. Everyone loves a good murder story – history is full of them, like the murder of Julius Caesar. Blood all over the place.

And there are war stories, thrillers, horror stories and comedies. That's the sort of history you'll find in this book. With a bit of luck you might even horrify your teacher!

Terrible Timeline

753 BC

Roman legend says Rome was founded by **Romulus**. The truth is that the early Romans were farmers living in a region called **Latium**.

509 BC

The Romans are fed up with their cruel king, **Tarquin**. They throw him out and rule themselves (that's called a Republic).

264 BC

First of the Punic Wars against the great enemy, Carthage (in North Africa).
Result: **Rome 1 Carthage 0**.

218 BC

Hannibal of Carthage attacks Rome with the help of elephants. He can't capture Rome but rampages round Italy terrorizing people.

THIS IS TERRIBLE. THAT ELEPHANT'S OFF-SIDE

HEY! THIS IS FUN!

202 BC

Scipio takes charge of the Roman Army and beats Hannibal. **Rome 2 Carthage 0**. The Roman farmers take over more and more land till they have the whole of Italy.

146 BC

Third War to wipe Carthage out forever. Game, set and match to Rome! The Romans get to like the idea of conquering people! They start on the rest of the world.

130 BC

By now the Romans have conquered Greece and most of Spain.

100 BC

Julius Caesar is born.

59 BC

Julius Caesar becomes Consul for the first time.

55 BC

Julius Caesar invades **Britain** for the first time because (he says) **a)** the Belgae of south Britain are helping the Gauls of north France to rebel against the Romans, and **b)** there is a wealth of tin, copper and lead to be found in Britain.

44 BC

Julius Caesar is elected dictator for life – then **murdered!**

AD 43

Claudius gives orders for the invasion of Britain ... again!

I'M OFF!

AD 60

One tribe, the Iceni, rebel. Queen **Boudica** leads them in massacres of Romans. Roman General Paulinus defeats her and **she poisons herself**.

AD 80

Julius Agricola completes the invasion (except for the Picts in Scotland).

AD 84

Agricola beats the Picts at Mons Graupius in Scotland.

AD 122

Hadrian starts building a wall across northern England to **keep out** the Picts.

AD 235–285

Fifty-year period with over 20 Roman emperors mainly because they keep getting **murdered**.

AD 313

Emperor Constantine allows Christian worship.

AD 380

Christianity becomes official religion of Rome.

AD 401

Roman troops are being withdrawn from Britain to defend Rome.

AD 410

Barbarian tribes from Germany begin attacks on the empire and Rome itself.

AD 476

The last Roman emperor of the western empire is forced to retire.

AD 1453

The empire of the east falls to the Turks. **End of the Roman Empire**.

The Rotten Roman Army

In the year AD 43 the Romans invaded Britain. The Roman Army didn't run all of Roman Britain. Once they'd won the battles they moved on to fight somewhere else. Towns were built in the beaten bits with Roman lords in charge. Just in case the Britons felt like revolting, the Romans let retired Roman soldiers settle in the land outside the towns – a circle of trusted men to warn of danger. And, if the battered Brits did give trouble then the army could get back quickly to help by marching along the new Roman roads.

Your teachers will tell you all about the legions and what they wore and how they lived. But they don't know everything.

TEST YOUR TEACHER...

Ask your teacher these questions.
Can they get more than 5 out of
10? Can you?

If you were a Roman soldier...
1 What would you wear under your
leather kilt?
a) nothing
b) underpants
c) fig leaves

2 Where would you drive on the
Roman roads?
a) on the right
b) down the centre
c) on the left

3 How long would you have to stay in the army once you joined?

a) 25 years

b) 5 years

c) the rest of your life

I'M A CENTURIAN CENTURIAN

4 Who could you marry?

a) your granny

b) no one

c) a Roman

5 Who paid for your uniform, weapons, food and burial?

a) the emperor

b) your granny

c) you paid for them yourself out of your wages

6 How tall did you have to be?

a) over 1.8 metres

b) between 1.6 and 1.8 metres

c) tall enough to touch your toes

7 What would you use instead of toilet paper?

a) a sponge on the end of a stick

b) your tunic

c) the daily newspaper

8 Your spear (pilum) had a 60-cm metal head that would snap off after it hit something. Why?

a) so the enemy couldn't pick up the spear and throw it back

b) so you could put the metal head in your pocket when you were marching

c) because the Roman armourers couldn't make the heads stay on

9 Why was one Roman Centurion called "Give me another"?

a) because he liked his soldiers to sing as they marched. When they'd finished one song he'd call out, "Give me another!"

b) because he was greedy. After eating a pig's head he'd cry out, Give me another!"

c) because he cruelly beat his soldiers so hard he smashed his canes and had to call out,

"GIVE ME ANOTHER!"

10 Why would the army doctor not notice your screams as he treated your wounds?

a) because he enjoyed making you suffer

b) because he was trained to carry on without caring about a soldier's cries

c) because the Romans only employed deaf men as doctors

Answers

1b. 2c (But they often barged straight down the middle of town streets in their chariots. They marched there too, trampling anyone who got in the way with their hob–nailed boots!). **3a. 4b** (But they often had wives outside of the camp). **5c. 6b.** (But this rule was sometimes broken when the army was desperate for men … and the men who were too small were might still have to work for the army even if they couldn't fight). **7a** (And you'd share it with everyone else in the public toilets! Sometimes you'd use a lump of moss, though, and that would be flushed away). **8a. 9c. 10b.**

The rottenly clever Roman Army

The Romans were the best army in the ancient world because they used something their enemies didn't. The Romans used their brains! Are you as brainy?

Here are some problems the Romans overcame. What would you have done if you'd faced these problems…

I Julius Caesar had a land army in Gaul (northern France). When the Veneti tribe there rebelled, they captured two Roman messengers and sailed off with them. Caesar quickly had ships built and followed. The Veneti were excellent sailors but poor fighters. Caesar needed a weapon that would stop the Veneti ships from sailing off while Roman soldiers climbed aboard. There was no gunpowder (for cannon or bullets). What simple (but very successful) weapon did the Romans make?

2 After the British Queen Boudica was beaten, the Romans were able to move into the fenlands of East Anglia. The grass was rich but the land was very wet. If the Romans tried to wade through the swamps, the local tribes ambushed them. Then a new general arrived from Italy's Pontine marshes. He showed the soldiers how to get through swamps without wading up to their waists in water. What did he teach them?

3 In the early days of the Roman Republic, the Romans came up against the Greek king, Pyrrhus. The Greeks would go into battle led by elephants.

The elephants would charge at the Romans, trample them and send them running. But the Romans learned quickly. At the battle of Beneventum they found a way to face an elephant charge ... and win! What would you do?

4 Some of the young men in the conquered lands did not want to fight in the Roman Army. It meant leaving their homes, farms and families to fight (and maybe die) in some distant corner of the world. The young men cut off the thumb of their right hand so they couldn't hold a sword. If they couldn't hold a sword then they wouldn't be expected to fight in the Roman Army. The Roman generals realized that all of these thumbless young men were trying to outwit them. What was their way of stopping this?

5 One day, Emperor Hadrian went to the public baths where his skin was carefully cleaned by slaves with scrapers. He saw an old man rubbing his back against a column. The old man was one of Hadrian's old soldiers. Hadrian asked why he was rubbing himself against the marble. The old man said it was because he couldn't afford a slave with a scraper. Hadrian gave the man slaves and money. BUT … next day the public baths were full of old men rubbing their backs against the marble! They were scrounging for a Hadrian handout! What would you do if you were Hadrian?

1 The Romans fixed hooked knives onto the ends of long poles. As they neared the Veneti ships, the Romans slashed the enemy ropes and sails to stop them sailing. They then climbed aboard the Veneti boats and captured the sailors. The leaders were executed and the sailors sold for slavery.

2 How to use stilts! They were a great success at first. Eventually the tribes of the fens learned to knock the Romans off the stilts and stab them as they fell. Ah, well, it seemed like a brilliant idea at the time!

3 The Roman front line split in two. The elephants charged harmlessly through the line.

They were too clumsy for the drivers to stop and turn. The helpless riders just kept going to the back of the Roman Army, where there were special troops waiting with long, sharp spears. They jabbed the elephants until the maddened creatures turned round and charged back again. The elephants flattened the Greek army, who weren't expecting them!

4 Cut off their heads! Anyone trying to avoid army service was sentenced to death. The young men soon learned this new law and decided to fight – possible death in war was better than certain death by execution. The Romans also branded or tattooed unwilling soldiers – if the soldier deserted, then he would have trouble hiding the fact that he was supposed to be in the army.

5 Hadrian simply told the old men to rub each other's backs!

Make the punishment fit the crime

If you think punishments at school are hard, then how would you like to have been in the Roman Army? The barbarian armies charged at the Romans like bulls at a matador – and we know who usually wins that contest. The Roman Army had "discipline". They did what they were told, every time. And if they didn't do as they were told – no matter how small the offence – they had to be punished. Try to guess which crime earned which punishment...

CRIME

PUNISHMENT

I LAZINESS

A. DECIMATION OF A UNIT – 1 MAN IN EVERY X IS EXECUTED

II FALLING ASLEEP ON DUTY

B. SLEEP OUTSIDE THE SAFTEY OF THE CAMP

III RUNNING AWAY IN A BATTLE

C. GET THE WORST FOOD – ROUGH BARLEY INSTEAD OF GOOD CORN

IV PUTTING YOUR UNIT IN DANGER

D. DEATH BY BEATING

V RUNNING AWAY WITH YOUR UNIT

E. DEATH BY STONING

I B. II C. III D. IV E (Your unit would throw the stones). **V A** (The unlucky one in ten was chosen by drawing lots.)

Let the reward fit the action

Of course there were good sides to being a Roman soldier too – otherwise no one would have wanted to join the army! The goodies were...

I The army took two parts of every seven you earned in wages and saved it for you. When you retired they gave you all your savings and a piece of land. You could retire in comfort ... if you lived long enough.

2 You could make extra wealth by robbing the countries you defeated. You could take money, animals or even living prisoners that you could sell for slaves.

3 For brave actions there were no medals – there were crowns:

a crown of oak leaves – for saving the life of a fellow citizen (Caesar won one at Mytilene when he was just 20 years old)

b a crown of plaited grass – for rescuing an army under siege

c a crown of gold – for being the first soldier over the wall of an enemy town.

Don't get sick!

Roman doctors knew how to…

BUT – Roman doctors didn't know about anaesthetics (to put you to sleep while they hacked you about!).

Roman doctors could make medicines to cure sickness. BUT – they had to mix them with honey to try to disguise the disgusting tastes.

"DID YOU KNOW?
A ROMAN LEGIONARY
ALWAYS WENT INTO
BATTLE WITH A FIRST–AID
KIT OF BANDAGES AND
HEALING HERBS?"

The Cut-Throat Celts

At one time the Celts had roamed round the world as much as the Romans did. One man put an end to all that the Roman emperor, Julius Caesar.

The Celts used to fight fiercely for their tribal chiefs. But the tribes often fought against each other when they should have been fighting together against Julius Caesar. They needed one strong leader to bring them all together. But when that leader arrived it was too late.

WE'LL GET RID OF THE ROMANS AFTER WE'VE POLISHED OFF YOU!

YEAH!

OH YEAH?

Vercingetorix was a Celtic chief who was just as clever as Caesar at fighting and leading. Would you have been as clever as Vercingetorix? Here are some of the problems he faced. Could you have solved them?

Vercingetorix v Caesar

1 You meet the chiefs of the tribes every day to plan your war against Caesar. One of the chiefs argues against you. What do you do about him?

a Say to him, "Look, my friend, we must all stick together if we want to beat the rotten Romans. So, please, trust me. Remember, united we stand but divided we fall."

b Get upset. Say, "If you're going to argue with me you can find yourselves another leader. I'll fight Caesar by myself. When I've beaten him I'll beat you next. You'll be sorry!"

WE HAD A BIT OF A FALLING OUT

c Don't get upset. Simply have his ears cut off and one of his eyes gouged out. Send him back to his tribe with the message, "This is what you get if you mess with Vercingetorix!"

2 Caesar is a long way from home and a long way from fresh supplies. The Romans need food for the soldiers and their horses. They are getting it from the Celtic towns in the region of the Bituriges tribe. What can you do to stop them?

a Tell the Bituriges' chief to burn his towns to the ground and send his people to live with other tribes.

b Tell the Bituriges' chief to destroy all the food in the towns but let the people stay.

c Tell the Bituriges' chief to burn his towns to the ground but move all the people to the capital city of Avaricum.

3 Your tactics are working. Caesar is getting desperate for food. He sets off for Avaricum, which is the region's grain depot. How can you defend Avaricum against Caesar's army?

a Build a wooden wall.

b Build a stone wall with a ditch in front.

c Build a brick wall.

4 Caesar begins to build towers on wheels to push up to the walls. When these towers reach the walls the Romans will let down a drawbridge at the top and swarm over your walls. What can you do?

a Build an even taller tower behind your walls and throw down fireballs on top of them.

A SIMPLE GUARD TOWER WOULD HAVE DONE

b Leave the town and attack Caesar's towers.

c Run away.

5 Caesar cannot get the towers near the walls because there is a ditch in front of the walls; He sends soldiers into the forest to chop down trees. He rolls the logs into the ditch and begins to fill it up. What can you do to stop the Romans filling the ditch?

a Dig a tunnel under your walls and set fire to the logs?

b Surrender.

c Send a raiding party out to steal the Roman axes so they can't chop down any more trees.

6 The Romans manage to get towers up to the walls. You would like to set fire to them but the clever Romans have covered them with leather, which doesn't catch fire very easily. What can you throw at them instead?

a dead horses.

b boiling fat and tar.

c cold water.

7 Despite your efforts the Romans reach the walls. They catch hold of the top of the wall with hooks, and swarm up the ropes attached to the hooks. What's the best defence against this?

a Throw the hooks back.

b Pull the hooks up and drag them inside your fort.

c Wait for the Romans to climb them and try to kill them as they reach the top.

8 During the Roman assault it begins to rain heavily. What do your defenders do?

a Run for shelter until the rain stops and hope the Romans do the same.

b Fight on and get wet.

c Ask the Romans for a ceasefire until the weather improves.

9 The Romans reach the streets of Avaricum. They begin slaughtering every man, woman and child in sight. What should Vercingetorix do?

a Give himself up.

b Fight to the death.

c Make sure his best fighting men escape through a back entrance.

10 Vercingetorix reaches the safety of Alesia. The Romans are following. You have a large army. What should you do with it?

a Send most of the army away to gather help from other Celtic tribes and keep just a few to defend Alesia.

b Keep all the soldiers in Alesia and hope that help will arrive.

c Leave the army in Alesia and go for help yourself?

Vercingetorix's ten Steps to Rome, or, the answers:

1c Vercingetorix could not afford to show any weakness or he'd be killed by the other Celtic chiefs. He could not plead (**1a**) or sulk (**1b**). He had to show he meant business and would make an example of anyone who opposed him (**1c**).

2c Vercingetorix made just one mistake. He couldn't destroy the supplies and leave the people in the towns (**2b**) – the warriors would not have fought if they knew the Romans had captured their wives and children. He should have destroyed the supplies AND the towns (**2a**). If you chose **2a**

then you'd have been a crueller but better leader than Vercingetorix! But the Bituriges were proud of Avaricum. They pleaded with Vercingetorix not to destroy it. He weakened and agreed (**2c**). From then on he was pretty well doomed.

3b Vercingetorix had fought the Romans for years and knew their way of fighting. They would have simply burned a wooden wall (**3a**) and battered down a brick wall (**3c**). The best wall was a solid stone wall with a ditch in front (**3b**).

4a Caesar wasn't put out by the solid walls of Avaricum. He began building towers. Vercingetorix expected this and didn't give up (**4c**). Of course, he didn't leave the safety of the town and attack the Romans in open battle (**4b**) because that's exactly what they wanted. He just ordered bigger towers to be built behind his own walls (**4a**).

5a Caesar could defeat the ditch by filling it with new logs. Vercingetorix couldn't stop him (**5c**) but didn't let it beat him (**5b**). The Bituriges were good iron miners and so could dig shafts. They dug one under the Roman logs and set fire to them (**5a**). This delayed the Roman attack ... but failed to stop it.

6b The Celtic soldiers knew that the only thing that would slow down the Roman towers wasn't anything solid (**6a**), but liquid, which would run through the joins in the Roman "umbrella". Cold water wasn't going to hurt them (**6c**) but boiling tar and oil would. This is what they did (**6b**).

7b The Romans were determined – and getting hungrier! They began to use grappling hooks to climb the walls. There was no point in throwing them back (**7a**) because the Romans would just try again at another spot. No one had been able to stop the Romans by trying to kill them at the top (**7c**) because there were just too many of them. Clever Vercingetorix devised the plan of hauling up the hooks and taking away the Roman weapons (**7b**)!

8a When a rain-storm hit Avaricum, all of Vercingetorix's cleverness was undone by the stupidity of his men. They should have fought on (**8b**). The Romans wouldn't let some rain stop them (**8c**) and it was no use expecting them to. The defenders ran for shelter (**8a**). The Romans leapt over the walls.

9c Vercingetorix knew that the battle for Avaricum was lost, but the war wasn't. He wasn't going to give up (**9a**). On the other hand there was no point in waiting to be killed (**9b**) when there were new Celtic armies waiting to fight. All he had to do was to escape with the soldiers and fight again (**9c**). Unfortunately, the women who were being left behind to be massacred didn't like the idea. Not surprising really! They began wailing and screaming. This gave the escape plan away to the Romans and they hurried to cut off the escape route. The Romans massacred 40,000 Avaricum people. Only Vercingetorix and 800 others escaped to fight another day.

10a Vercingetorix reached the safety of Alesia with a new large army. If he'd tried to keep the army with him (**10b**) they'd have eaten the supplies in no time and starved to death before help arrived. He couldn't get to all the dozens of tribes himself to get help (**10c**) so he sent his troops to different Celtic tribes and kept just enough to defend the town (**10a**).

It almost worked. A huge Celtic army arrived. But the Romans had built a ring of defences round the town. The soldiers in Alesia couldn't get out. The new Celtic army couldn't get in. They gave up and went away.

Vercingetorix was trapped. He gave himself up to his own people and said they could do what they needed. The Romans wanted Vercingetorix alive – that was how the Celts delivered him. In 45 BC he was paraded through the streets of Rome ... then executed. The Celts on the continent were crushed. They survived mainly in the islands off the shores of Europe. The British Islands. If Caesar wanted to finish them off, then he had to invade Britain ... which he did.

That's why it's thought that the defeat of Vercingetorix led to the Roman invasion of Britain! If Vercingetorix had only destroyed Avaricum (as in **2a**) then we might never have had a Roman Britain!

Heads you win, heads you lose

Heads were popular with the Celtic race who were Rome's great enemy. Here are ten horrible brainless facts...

1 In 500 BC, the British tribes believed that the head had magical powers. They thought that severed heads could look into the future and give warnings, especially if they were in groups of three.

2 Rotting human heads were stuck on poles at the entrance to a hill fort.

3 Heads could be thrown into a lake or river as a gift to the gods.

4 After a battle the Celts rode from the battlefield with the heads of enemies dangling from the necks of their horses.

5 The heads might then be nailed to the walls of their houses.

6 Sometimes they were kept in in cedar oil and taken out years later to show off to visitors. A Roman visitor said that the Britons would not part with their lucky heads for their weight in gold.

7 The Celtic Boii Tribe of the Po Valley (Northern Italy) took skulls and covered them in gold. They would then be used as cups!

8 Heads appeared in many ornaments of stone, metal or wood and paintings. Severed heads could be seen staring at you from the surface of tiles, pots, sword hilts, chariot fittings and even bucket handles!

9 Because the gods were more powerful than humans, they often had more heads. An Irish goddess, Ellen, had three heads! The druids had to keep her fed with sacrifices to stop her coming out of her underworld cave and ravaging the land.

10 The Britons even told stories about the magical power of the head. Many legends involved severed heads. One story is the Welsh legend of Bran the Blessed…

BIG BRAN'S NOGGIN NICKED!

Some treacherous troublemaker has taken Britain's greatest treasure!

Yesterday the London burial place of Bran the Blessed was robbed. The great warrior's head was later found to be missing, along with another two skulls from the graveyard. The authorities are looking for a man with three heads!

Magical

As all our readers will know, the head of Bran the Blessed was the most magical article in the whole of Britain. Eight years ago Bran was mortally wounded in a bloody battle with an Irish king. As he lay dying he ordered the seven surviving soldiers to cut off his head and carry it with them. This they did and they found themselves in the afterlife as the guest of Bran – even though they weren't dead!

Then one warrior disobeyed one of Big Bran's orders. He opened a forbidden door. The warriors were heaved out of heaven. But, before they went, one of them tucked Brian's head up his tunic. And so it returned to earth. The head was buried in London, where it would guard Britain against evil for ever more.

Reward

Now it has been stolen there's no knowing what might happen. The *Daily Headline News* is offering a reward for information leading to its return.

Otherwise Britain will be heading for disaster!

Suffering slaves

"DID YOU KNOW?
THE ROMANS SOMETIMES TREATED SLAVES
BRUTALLY IN THEIR CONQUERED TERRITORIES
AND IN ROME ITSELF. IN AD 157 THE ROMAN
WRITER APULEIUS DESCRIBED LIFE IN A ROTTEN
ROMAN FLOUR MILL... THE SLAVES WERE POOR,
SKINNY THINGS. THEIR SKIN WAS BLACK
AND BLUE WITH BRUISES, THEIR
BACKS WERE COVERED WITH
CUTS FROM THE WHIP. THEY
WORE RAGS, NOT CLOTHES, AND
HARDLY ENOUGH TO KEEP THEM
DECENT. THEY HAD A BRAND
MARK BURNED INTO THEIR
FOREHEAD AND HALF OF THEIR HAIR WAS
SHAVED OFF. THEY WORE CHAINS
AROUND THEIR ANKLES."

A slave revolt was led by Spartacus at a gladiator school near Naples. The slaves formed a huge army and terrorized the area for a couple of years. At last a Roman army defeated them. Over 6,000 slaves were crucified along the side of the main road from Capua to Rome.

Roman Revenge

One of the great heroes of the British tribes was Caratacus of the Catuvellauni tribe (north-west of London). While many tribal leaders were making peace with the Romans, Caratacus went on fighting. In the end he was defeated, of course. But he was still a hero.

That was one big difference. The Romans loved winners. The Britons seemed to love losers. The other difference was that the Romans learned from their mistakes. The Britons didn't.

It isn't likely that Caratacus could write. But, if he could, and if he kept a diary, would it have looked like this…?

Summer of AD43 Kent

Disaster! I can't believe it! After two days of battle the Romans have defeated us. All we had to do was to stop them crossing the ~~Medw~~ River Medway. There's only one bridge over the Medway. All we had to do was sit tight on the northern end, wait for the Romans to cross it, then cut them into pieces…

... We'd have killed them in their
thousands. We would! But what did
they do ??? They cheated !!! They
sent troops upstream, they crossed
where the water was shallow and
attacked us from the back. That's not
fair, is it?

Of course, we could have run them down
with our chariots. We could! But what did
they do? They cheated again!
They shot our horses. That's not fair, is it?
They even killed my brother, Togodumnus.
Poor, stupid Toggy. He should have done
what I did. Retreated. Like dad always
said, "He who fights and runs away, lives
to fight another day."

So, I'm alive and next time I'll stuff
those rotten Romans !!!!

Late Summer of AD43 - Dorset

Disater! Again! The Romans are marching west. They're taking our hill-forts one after another. Of course, they dont fight ~~fair~~ fair. ~~It~~ They dont fight man to man ~~to~~ and let us kill them....

No. They shoot at our defenders with iron-tipped arrows. Hundreds at a time from some big machine. They drive us off the walls then swarm in after we've taken shelter.

They've taken 20 hill-forts that way. I never thought I'd live to see the day they'd take the mighty Maiden Castle. In fact I nearly didn't live to see today! I just managed to retreat in time. He who fights and runs away.... But I'll stay in England. They'll never drive me into Wales.. Never!!

The other leaders are all surrendering, making peace and getting fat. But they wont get a hero like me. Not like they got poor old Toggy... ~~Next~~ Next time I'll get them...

Summer of AD48 - Wales

Who is the greatest British leader??
Carataeus. Me! Alright, so I'm stuck in the
wild, wet Welsh mountains. But every now and
then I lead a raid on some Roman troops
and crack a few rotten Roman heads.

Actually it's rather hard to crack a Roman
head. They wear these metal helmets. That's not
fair, that's not. Some people might even call
it cheating!

They'd like to drive me up to North Wales
and into the Irish Sea. Well, there is absolutely
NO chance of that. My men will fight to ~~the~~
the death (Not my death of course. They
need me alive to lead them)

I'll end up in North Wales over my warrior's
dead bodies!!!

North
Wales

Nth England

Welsh
Mountains

Dorset   Kent

North Wales - AD51

Disaster! Again!!! I never thought I'd see the day when the Romans would take a fort like Llanymynech. But they did. I still can't believe it. They couldn't attack Llanymynech from the back because that's a steep mountain face. They couldn't attack it from the front because that's the river Vrynwy and the front wall of the fort

But they did it! They crossed the river then came to the wall. We were pouring spears and stones and ~~and~~ arrows down on their heads. We should have massacred them...

So, what did they do? They cheated, us usual. They put their sheilds over their heads and came close together. The shields formed a solid wall over them. (They copied this from a Roman animal with a shell called a "tortoise" or something)

Our weapons just bounced off their "shell" and the Romans just kept coming till everyone was captured. The rotten Romans even took my family! I was lucky to escape. He who fights and runs away...... Still, next time I'll get them. I'm going to join forces with Queen Cartimandua of the Brigantes up near York ....

They're the biggest tribe outside of Roman rule. With me to lead them we'll chase the Romans all the way back to Rome. And they can take their tortoises with them.

I even hear old Claudius brought some huge grey monsters called elephants with him. They can take them back too!!! This time next year I'll be in Rome!!!

North England - later in AD 51

Life with Queen Cartimandua is great! I don't even miss my poor captured family. The beautiful Carti obviously fancies me. Can't blame her really. Me being the greatest British hero ever seen.

Loads of food. Better than living like an outlaw in the hills. And loads of wine. Lovely stuff. The very besht Roman wine. I wonder where she gets it from?

And she's even decorating me with chains. Chains on my wrists. Chains on my ankles. I fink that Carti loves me to show mush she wantsh to keep me here forever!!! I'm very shleepy now.

Nighty night Carti dear!

Next day

My head hurts. And worse. Much worse I'm a prisoner. I've found out where that treacherous, ugly, vicious, lying Queen gets her Roman wine from. She gets it from the Romans !!! And what does she give the Romans in return?

Me! I've been handed over to the Romans. They're ~~not~~ taking me back to Rome. It's curtains for Caratacus! I said I'd be in Rome within a year, I never thought it would be in chains. It's a disaster! They'll execute me for sure. Me the greatest living British hero. I'm not afraid to die of course... I just don't want to be there when it happens.

Next week - middle of the English Channel

I think I'm going to be sea-s...

Next month - Rome

What a place! These Romans really know how to treat a hero! Met old Claudius the emperor. Messy little weedy fellow. Dribbles and slobbers and limps about the place. But a very powerful man. Most important man in the world I reckon. And he spoke to me! (I didn't understand a word, of course, because he was blabbering away in Latin. But I could tell he was pleased to see me!)

Claudi gave an order and my chains were cut off. I thought, Aha! This is it! ~~You're~~ You're for the chop, Caratacus. But no! They treated me like a hero. They even said I was free to live in Rome. I think I might just do that. There are huge buildings all made of stone and marble. I've never seen anything like it.

Who wants to live in cold wet Britain in a draughty wooden hut? Not me! After all, I am the greatest British hero ever. I reckon I've earned an easy life with my old mate Claudi. Maybe the rotten Romans aren't so rotten after all !!!

The diary might be made up, but the facts are about right. Caratacus arrived in Rome and told the Romans that they could only have great victories if they had great warriors (like himself) to fight against. "If you execute me, then all your glory will be forgotten," he warned them. Claudius agreed and released him.

But Caratacus was still puzzled when he saw the wealth of Rome. "When you Romans have all this, why do you want our poor huts?" Good question.

Meanwhile, back in Britain, the treacherous Cartimandua stayed in power (with Roman help) for another 15 years. Then her husband attacked her and kicked her out. The Romans really did take the British forts with ease. The Romans made mistakes. But they didn't usually make the same mistake twice. That's what made them so successful.

MAYBE THEY WERE TRAITORS. WHATEVER THE REASON THEIR CARVED HEADS WERE WALLED UP IN THIS ROOM TO BE FORGOTTEN. BUT ONE BODY WAS FOUND IN THE TOMB — THE BODY OF THE FAMILY CAT!"

WHOSE FUNERAL IS THIS?

Rotten Roman Leaders

Julius Caesar was one of the greatest Roman leaders. He was so great he was murdered ... by his friend! Rome had been run as a "republic" for many years. That is to say the important people in Rome decided what to do. Then Julius Caesar became so powerful there was a fear that he'd take over. The people thought he wanted to become "King of the Romans".

The last king they'd had was a disaster. His name was Tarquinius Superbus who lived in the 5th century BC. He took away certain rights of Romans and was the rottenest Roman of the time.

Was it true that Caesar wanted to be crowned king? And would he get to be as bad as Tarquinius? If so, it would be better to kill him now! This is how it happened…

Caesar's sticky end

1 Caesar had himself elected "Dictator for life" … that was just another way of saying the dreaded word "King"!

2 Caesar started wearing red boots! Only a king wore red boots.

3 At a festival, Mark Antony, Caesar's friend, offered Caesar a diadem – a small crown. Caesar took it off – a sign that he didn't want to be king, perhaps? The crowds cheered when he took it off. But did Caesar and Mark Antony set this up to find out how the people felt? What if the people had cheered when the crown had been put on?

4 Caesar was due to speak to the Senate (the Roman parliament) on 15 March, 44 BC. Straight after his speech he was due to lead his troops into battle. During a war he'd be surrounded by his soldiers. No one could kill him then. If he was to die then he had to die on 15 March.

5 Caesar was a great believer in "fate" – if he was going to die then there was nothing he could do to change that. A fortune-teller told Caesar not to go to the Senate on 15 March. It didn't stop him.

6 Caesar's wife asked him not to go to the Senate that day. She'd had terrible nightmares and a feeling that something bad would happen. That didn't stop him.

7 Caesar felt ill on the morning of 15 March and was almost too ill to attend the Senate … he was worse by the time he left!

8 The killers chose Brutus as their leader. Brutus was one of the most popular men in Rome. He was famous for being honest. If he led the killing then the people of Rome would know the murderers were "honest" – that they did it for the good of the people.

9 On the evening of 14 March someone asked Caesar, "What sort of death would you like?" Caesar answered, "A sudden one." He got his wish.

10 Plutarch told the grim and gory story…

"WHEN CAESAR ENTERED THE SENATE THE SENATORS ALL STOOD UP AS A SIGN OF RESPECT. SOME OF BRUTUS' GANG SLIPPED BEHIND CAESAR'S CHAIR WHILE OTHERS CAME TO MEET HIM. CIMBER GRABBED CAESAR'S ROBE WITH BOTH HANDS AND PULLED IT FROM HIS NECK. THIS WAS THE SIGNAL FOR THE ATTACK…

CASCA STRUCK THE FIRST BLOW.
HIS KNIFE MADE A WOUND IN CAESAR'S
NECK, BUT NOT A SERIOUS ONE, SO THAT
CAESAR COULD STILL TURN AROUND,
GRAB THE KNIFE, AND HOLD ON.
THE WATCHERS WERE HORRIFIED . THEY
DIDN'T DARE RUN AWAY OR HELP
CAESAR OR EVEN MAKE A SOUND .
EACH ASSASSIN BARED HIS DAGGER NOW.
THEY ALL CLOSED IN ON CAESAR IN A
CIRCLE. THEY PUSHED HIM THIS WAY
AND THAT, LIKE A WILD BEAST
SURROUNDED BY HUNTERS.
BRUTUS STABBED CAESAR IN
THE GROIN. ABOVE ALL CAESAR HAD
TRUSTED BRUTUS.
SOME SAY CAESAR DEFENDED HIMSELF
AGAINST ALL THE REST — BUT WHEN HE
SAW BRUTUS COMING AT HIM WITH A
DAGGER, HE PULLED HIS ROBE OVER HIS
HEAD AND SANK DOWN.

THE ATTACKERS PUSHED CAESAR
AGAINST THE STATUE OF HIS
OLD ENEMY, POMPEY. THE STATUE
BECAME DRENCHED WITH BLOOD.
CAESAR RECEIVED 23 WOUNDS.
MANY OF THE ASSASSINS WOUNDED EACH
OTHER AS THEY FOUGHT TO STICK SO
MANY KNIVES INTO ONE BODY. "

The killers made one big mistake. They didn't kill Mark Antony at the same time. "Honest" Brutus said it would be wrong. They were only out to stop wicked Caesar from becoming king. But it was Mark Antony who led a campaign of vengeance that destroyed the killers. Brutus committed suicide when he was defeated by Mark Antony at the battle of Philippi in 42 BC.

Caesar had left most of his fortune to his grandnephew, Octavian. Young Octavian became the sort of dictator that Caesar wanted to be. The thing the Romans feared – rule by one all-powerful man – had returned. And some of the emperors that followed were a hundred times worse than Julius Caesar!

In fact, some of the Roman Emperors were pretty weird. Here are the Rottenest Romans of all…

EMPEROR TIBERIUS
Ruled: AD 14–37

Favourite saying: "I don't care if they hate me ... as long as they obey me!" (Know any teachers like that?)

Nastiest habit: Breaking the legs of anyone who disobeyed him.

Rottenest act: Tiberius needed a holiday. "I think I'll take a break!" he announced. As the servants scuttled off to find their shinpads he cried, "A holiday, I mean. A short break on the island of Capri off the south coast of Italy would be very nice."

He had only been there a few days when a humble Capri fisherman caught a large crab and a huge mullet fish. The poor man decided that it would make a wonderful gift for the visiting emperor. The cliff was steep and there was no track. The mullet was heavy. The fisherman struggled for an hour and finally reached the top.

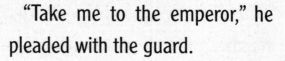

"Take me to the emperor," he pleaded with the guard.

"The emperor wishes to be left alone today," the guard said, shaking his head.

"It's the biggest mullet I've ever caught!" the fisherman said proudly. "The gods meant it for the emperor. Tell the emperor I must see him!"

The guard shrugged. It was a boring life, standing on the top of the cliff watching the gulls. The emperor might order him to break the fisherman's legs. "I'll see what the emperor says," he smirked.

Five minutes later he returned and said with a grin. "The emperor will see you now."

The poor little man dragged the huge fish into the emperor's room. "You'll be sorry," the guard muttered.

As the fisherman stepped through the door two huge guards grabbed his arms. "I've brought a gift for the emperor!" he squeaked.

Tiberius stepped forward. "You disturbed my rest you smelly little man!" he snarled.

"It's the fish, your worship!" the fisherman cried.

"No!" the emperor jeered. "That fish smells sweeter than you. Guards!"

"Sir?"

"Sweeten the little man. Rub that fish over his body!"

"It was a present ... ouch! Mullet scales are very rough!" he screamed.

The guard scrubbed the rough skin over the fisherman's face till the skin was scraped off and his face left raw and bleeding. The guard smiled as he stripped the skin off the fisherman's chest.

"Ahh! Oooh!" the man wailed.

"Enough!" the emperor snapped. The guards let the fisherman fall to the floor where he lay groaning and muttering something through his bleeding lips.

"What did you say?" Tiberius growled.

"I just said thank the gods I didn't bring you that big crab I caught this morning," the little man burbled.

The emperor's eyes lit up with evil glee. "Go to this man's house and fetch the crab," he chuckled.

The guard nodded. As he left the emperor's room he winked at the sobbing fisherman. "I told you that you'd be sorry."

And after being scrubbed with the sharp shell of a crab the little man was so sorry that he wished he'd never been born.

Sticky end: Tiberius died at the age of 78, probably suffocated by his chief helper. The Roman people went wild with joy!

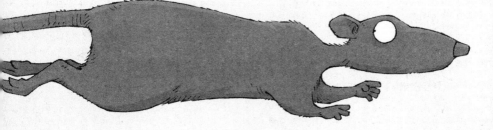

CALIGULA

Ruled: AD **37–41**

Favourite sayings: To his friends at a banquet, "It has just occurred to me that I only have to give one nod and your throats will be cut."

To the guards of a row of criminals, "Kill every man between that one with the bald head and that one over there."

To his people, "Rome is a city of necks just waiting for me to chop."

To everyone who would listen, "I am a god."

Nastiest habit: "His little jokes". At a sacrifice ceremony he was given a hammer which would knock out the beast to be sacrificed. The priest was waiting to cut the beast's throat. Caligula hit the priest over the head instead!

Rottenest act: Caligula loved to organize huge killing festivals with loads of spectators. There were fights to the death between gladiators, and fights with wild animals. But the wild animals had to be kept alive until the day of the contest. Caligula was shocked at the cost of the raw meat needed to feed the animals. So he found a cheap supply of meat ... he fed criminals to them!

Daftest act: He made his dear friend Incitatus a consul – so Incitatus became one of the most powerful rulers in the Roman Empire. So? So, Incitatus was his favourite horse!

Sticky end: One of his trusted guards stabbed him to death. Others went to the palace where they killed his wife and child.

CLAUDIUS

Ruled: AD **41–54**

Favourite saying: "Kk-k-k-k-k- … er … execute him!"

Nastiest habit: Watching criminals being tortured and men being executed by being flogged to death.

Rottenest act: Claudius discovered his wife was a bit of a flirt and had wild parties with her friends. Claudius not only had her executed but 300 party friends went too.

Sticky end: His niece, Agrippina, poisoned him with mushrooms.

NERO

Ruled: AD **54–68**

Favourite sayings: He played the lyre very badly but people told him he was brilliant. The Greeks were particularly creepy about telling him he was good. "Only the Greeks are worth my genius," he would say.

When he knew he had to die all he could say was, "What a loss I shall be to the art of music!"

Nastiest habit: Murdering people. He had his half-brother, Britannicus, poisoned. Actually, Britannicus had a food taster who ate and drank a tiny bit of every dish that the Emperor was going to eat. If the food was poisoned, the taster would die first. The taster drank some hot wine and passed it over to the emperor. The taster was fine. The wine was "safe" to drink. But Britannicus complained that the wine was too hot and ordered water to cool it. Then he drank it ... and died. The cold water had been poisoned!

PHEW!

Nero had his first wife, Octavia, murdered. Her head was sent to Nero's new girlfriend, Poppaea. But then he murdered Poppaea, too.

Nero had Christians persecuted cruelly…

• They would be tied to a post, covered in tar and set alight.

• They would be covered in animal skins and thrown to hungry, wild dogs.

• They were crucified in large numbers.

Rottenest act: Agrippina had poisoned Claudius and now her son, Nero, was emperor. She thought she could rule the empire through her weak and wicked son.

Nero had other ideas. His mother was always interfering – stopping his meeting with his girlfriend, Acte, because she wasn't royal. Agrippina had to go.

First he made up their row over Acte. Then he invited mum to join him at a party on the Bay of Naples. Agrippina was happy to accept, glad to be friends

with her son once more.

Nero sent a boat to pick her up. A special boat with special oarsmen. For the boat was designed to fall apart at sea and the oarsmen were instructed not to let Agrippina return alive. The boat set off on a beautiful starry night.

But the boat didn't fall apart. There were heavy weights on the wooden canopy over Agrippina's seat. At the right moment they were to crash through the canopy, kill Agrippina and fall through the bottom of the boat to sink it. Everyone would say the boat hit a rock. Sad accident. Poor Nero, losing his loving mother.

That's what was meant to happen. But, when the weights fell through the roof they killed Agrippina's

friend. Agrippina and her other friend, Aceronnia escaped ... and the boat didn't sink!

The oarsmen tried to rock the boat to capsize it. That's when Aceronnia did a very brave thing. She began to cry out, Save me! I am Agrippina, the emperor's mother! I am Agrippina!"

And in the darkness the oarsmen believed her. They battered her to death with their oars while the real Agrippina slipped over the side and escaped back to her palace. She sent a message to Nero saying what a lucky escape she'd had.

Nero was furious. He decided to make sure the next time. He sent two murderers to her palace. Agrippina thought they'd come from Nero to find out if she was all right!

As the first one battered her with a club she realized her mistake. When the other drew his sword she bared her stomach and invited him to stab her where the ungrateful Nero had come from. He did.

Nero reported that she had killed herself!

Sticky end: When he knew that the Roman Army had deserted him and rebels were coming to arrest him, he placed a sword to his throat. One of his friends gave him a push. The arresting officer arrived as he bled to death.

Ten funny fact about Roman emperors

1 Emperor Caligula's real name was Gaius. Caligula was just a nickname meaning "little boot". This was because he liked dressing up and playing at being a soldier from a very early age.

2 Caligula wanted to copy Julius Caesar and invade Britain. In AD 40 he went to the Roman base in Boulogne (in northern France) where he set sail to lead the invasion. He turned back when he saw that no one wanted to follow him!

3 Augustus Caesar was one of the kinder emperors. But even he had his moments – the murder of Julius Caesar really upset him. As Suetonius said, "Augustus showed no mercy to his beaten enemies.

He sent Brutus's head to Rome to be thrown at the feet of Caesar's statue."

4 Julius Caesar gave us our modern calendar. The early Romans had 12 months plus a 13th month that was added every four years. In 46 BC Caesar gave us the 12-month, 365-day year with the 29-day February leap year.

5 Emperor Heliogabalus enjoyed the hobby of collecting cobwebs ... by the ton!

OF ALL MY BELGIAN COBWEBS THIS IS MY FAVOURITE

6 Honorius loved chickens. His favourite chicken was called Rome. He was hiding in his country mansion, safe from the invading army of Goths. When the city of Rome was overrun by Alaric and his army of Goths, a messenger arrived to say, "Rome is lost!" Honorius was heart-broken…

…until someone told him the messenger meant the capital city and not the hen.

7 Nero enjoyed the cruel "circuses" so much that he had to take part. He was dressed in the skins of wild animals and locked in a cage. The human victims were tied to stakes in the arena. Nero's cage was opened. He leapt out and attacked the victims.

8 When Emperor Pertinax was murdered there wasn't just one person to take his place. Two men claimed the throne. Both men thought it would be useful to have the support of the emperor's praetorian guard – so they tried to outbid each other for it. Julianus won. He made an offer of 25,000 sesterces (Roman money) to each man. Unfortunately he couldn't afford to pay all the men in all the Roman armies across the world. They attacked and threw him out after just 66 days on the throne. The money he spent on bribing the emperor's guards was wasted – they were easily tricked into giving up their weapons.

9 In the 50 years between AD 235 and AD 285 there were about 20 emperors. Most of them were there a short time, murdered and replaced by the murderer who was murdered and replaced by the murderer, and so on. Some of the senior Romans refused to become emperor at this time – not surprising really!

10 Septimius had particularly nasty family problems. He had two sons, Caracalla and Geta. Caracalla was allowed to become joint emperor when he was just 13. Caracalla had his father-in-law murdered, then set off with his father and brother to conquer Scotland. During the campaign,

Caracalla threatened to kill his father – but didn't. Old Septimius died in York and his dying words to his sons were, "Do not disagree with each other." Fat chance. Within a year Caracalla had brother Geta murdered. Caracalla was sole emperor at last. He kept the throne for five years, then … no prizes for guessing what happened to him. Yes, he was murdered.

❝DID YOU KNOW? JULIUS CAESAR PASSED BURIAL LAWS FOR THE PEOPLE WHO LIVED IN THE NEW TOWNS BUILT IN THE ROMAN EMPIRE

"NO ONE MAY BRING, BURN OR BURY A DEAD PERSON WITHIN THE BOUNDARIES OF THE TOWN."
"NO CREMATORIUM SHALL BE BUILT WITHIN HALF A MILE OF A TOWN."

(BURIAL SITES HAD TO BE EITHER OUTSIDE THE CITY WALLS OR JUST INSIDE. CAESAR WANTED A PERFECT TOWN FULL OF GRAND BUILDINGS AND FRESH AIR FOR HIS FAITHFUL FOLLOWERS.)"

Rotten Roman Childhood

Children had a tough time in the age of the rotten Romans from the moment they were born. One writer, Soranus, described how each new-born child was laid on the earth and allowed to cry for a while before it was washed and clothed. Only the fit survived.

Some of the Germans in the Roman Empire gave their new-born children an even worse test. They dunked the child in cold water. If the baby came out purple with the cold or shivering then it was a weakling – it wasn't worth bringing up so it was left to die!

Girls were named eight days after they were born – boys on the ninth day. Girls would usually take their father's name – but change the "-us" on the end to "-a".

So the daughter of Julius became Julia, the daughter of Claudius was Claudia, Flavius was the father of Flavia and so on.

Children would probably have "pet names" or nicknames. One girl was known as "Trifosa" – that means "delicious"!

The Celt names had their own meanings…

- Boudica meant "Victory"
- Cartimandua meant "White Filly"
- Grata meant "Welcome"

Then, if you survived your birth, and you could live with your name, you had to face the terrors of the rotten Roman schools…

Suffering schoolchildren – the good, the bad and the awful

Good: Schools cost parents money, so only the parents who could afford it sent their children. If you were poor you could miss going to school altogether.

Bad: Slave children didn't go to school. They were born slaves and belonged to the master.

Awful: Poor children missed school but had to work twice as hard for parents. If you didn't your parents might just decide to sell you! It was illegal to sell free children as slaves – but this didn't stop poor parents from doing it. There was not much chance of their being caught.

Good: Education was divided rather as it is today into primary, secondary and college.

Bad: Most children only went as far as primary.

Awful: For laziness in primary school you'd get the cane, or a beating if the teacher didn't have a cane handy. One poet described his bullying teacher like this…

Good: Primary schools usually had just 10 to 12 children.

Bad: That was not enough to pay a teacher's wage. So the poor teacher had another job – maybe in a workshop.

Awful: The Romans didn't have the figure zero. That made sums rottenly difficult to teach. Ask your teacher, "Can you add LXXXVIII and XII?" (The answer is "C")

Good: At least schoolchildren had their own goddess. Her name was Minerva. The holiday for the goddess was in March. After the holiday the school year began.

Bad: Each child had to provide their own wax tablets and stylus (sharp pen to scratch letters into the wax), their pen and ink, their paper rolls and abacus (counting frame).

Awful: For a serious offence in the secondary school – a flogging with a leather whip while other pupils held you down.

Good: Schools closed every ninth day for the market – it was probably too noisy to teach on market days.

Bad: Primary schools were pretty boring. You'd study mainly the three 'Rs' – reading, 'riting and 'rithmetic.

Awful: At secondary school you had to study mega-boring grammar and literature, with some geography and, of course, horrible history! By the time you got to college you had to study for public speaking – the Romans believed that good talkers made good leaders. (Do you agree?)

WHO WROTE THAT!

HISTORY HORRIBILIS

A grim life for girls

Through most periods of history it's been harder being a woman than being a man. It was no different in Roman Britain…

1 Roman girls were lucky … if they lived!

"If you give birth to a boy, look after it – but if it is a girl then let it die!"
   (Letter from Hilarion to his wife.)

2 Men weren't happy with the idea of an educated woman. "I hate a woman who reads", wrote Juvenal in the 1st century AD.

3 Roman women had to be "controlled" from an early age. They were given a lucky charm at birth. Why? Because they didn't have a man of their own to protect them. When a baby girl was eight days old she was taken to a special ceremony. A gold or leather heart was hung around her neck. She would keep it throughout her childhood.

4 When a Roman girl was 14 she was ready for marriage. Who said so? Her father. A husband would be chosen for her. Who chose? Her father. What if the girl didn't like her father's choice? Bad luck. She'd have to marry him anyway.

5 On the evening before the wedding a special event took place. The girl placed all her toys and childhood clothes on the altar of the Lares – the household gods. She also took off her lucky charm – she had a husband to protect her now.

6 The bride always wore a white woollen tunic. It was held at the waist with a woollen belt tied in a special knot. She wore a bright yellow cloak and sandals. Her head was covered with a flame-coloured veil.

7 Roman women wore make-up. They used chalk to whiten their necks because a pale skin was supposed to be a sign of beauty.

8 If a woman's lips and cheeks weren't red enough then they would use a reddish earth called ochre.

9 Women were expected to remove hair from their legs as well as from under their arms. They rubbed hair off with a stone or used a cream to dissolve it and it's a wonder the creams didn't dissolve the skin too! One hair-remover consisted of the blood of a wild she-goat mixed with sea-palm and powdered viper. Then, if you wanted to stop the hair growing back again, you would have to rub on the blood of a hare.

10 If a girl's eyebrows weren't dark enough then she might have used a metallic stuff called antimony. No antimony? Then girls used ashes! Imagine walking around with mud on your face, chalk on your neck and ashes on your eyebrows. If you got carried away you'd look more like a scarecrow.

Rotten Roman stories

The Romans knew some pretty rotten stories. Stories of gods, graves and guts. Their own gods were a bit boring. But then they heard the stories of the Greek gods. Those gods were much more like interesting people. So the Romans pinched the Greek legends and made them their own. Stories like that of Prometheus...

The Eagle has landed ... again ... and again ... and again...

The fat, feathered fiend landed on the rock and looked at the man who lay chained to it. The bird's beak was as hooked as a hairpin. His great golden eyes glinted in the harsh sun. "Cor! Stone the crows! What a tasty sight!" he croaked. If he'd had lips he would have licked them. Instead he licked his beak.

The young prisoner lifted his head wearily. He was a handsome young man with nothing on but a loin cloth. He squinted through the fierce sun and glared at the bird. "Push off," he snapped.

The bird hopped from one hot foot to the other. Hey! That's no way to speak to me! I'll have you know I'm an eagle – king of the birds!"

"Sorry, I'm sure," the man sneered. "I should have said, 'push off, your highness'."

The eagle shrugged. "No need to be offensive. I'm only doing my job. And a bird's gotta do what a bird's gotta do!"

"And I'm tired of every sparrow on Mount Olympus stopping off here to gawp and stare," the prisoner spat.

The bird breathed in deeply and ruffled its breast feathers importantly. "I am here on a mission. Some old geezer at the top of the mountain sent me."

"The gods live at the top of the mountain," the man said.

"Yeah, well some old god sent me, then. Big guy with long white hair and a bushy great beard."

"Zeus!"

"Bless you ... anyway, he said, 'Fly down there and you'll see young Prometheus chained to a rock,'" the eagle went on.

"That's me! You've brought me the news that the great god Zeus has forgiven me? I'm to be set free?"

"Nah! The old guy told me to fly down here, and eat your liver."

"Eat my liver?" the young god groaned.

"Well, I didn't argue, did I?" the eagle chuckled.
"I like a nice bit of fresh liver. Specially when its
fried with a few onions."

"You'll kill me!" Prometheus cried.

"Nah! You're immortal. You'll 'liver' long time yet!
Heh! Heh! Heh!" the bird cackled.

The god blinked as sweat ran into his eyes. "You'll hurt me," he sniffed.

"Can't be helped," the bird croaked and took a step towards his victim. "You must have done something pretty bad to deserve this!"

Prometheus sighed and looked towards the sun. "Once I could move through the air, just like you. One day I flew up to the sun itself. I brought its fire back down to earth."

"Good thing too – otherwise I'd have to eat your liver raw," the eagle chuckled nastily.

The young god went on, "I gave it to the humans to use."

"Sounds fair enough to me," the eagle admitted.

"Ah, but Zeus had told me not to give fire to the humans. He was furious. My punishment is to be chained to this mountainside.

"And to have your liver eaten," the eagle reminded him.

"Must you?" Prometheus groaned.

"Cor, stone the crows. You're supposed to be a hero, ain't you? Well, stop whingeing and let me get me dinner."

The bird lunged forward and Prometheus screamed.

When it was over the bird gripped the dripping liver in its talons and opened its wings. The mountain air lifted it gently off the mountainside and the eagle soared upwards. "See you tomorrow, Prommy!" it cried.

"Tomorrow!" Prometheus screamed. "What bit of me are you going to eat tomorrow?"

"Same again!" the eagle cawed. "That's the worst bit of the punishment. Your liver grows back. I'll come back tomorrow and eat it again … and the next day … and the next … until the end of time! Bye for now!"

Prometheus twisted his head to look at his side. There wasn't a mark to show the eagle's work.

And every day the eagle returned. Day after day, month after month and year after year. Until one day…

"Hello there, Prom!" the eagle called happily as it clattered down onto the sun-warmed rock.

"Hello, Eddie," Prometheus grinned.

The eagle took a step back. "Er … you look happy this morning, Prom!"

The young god nodded happily. There was a gleam of pure nastiness in his eyes. Suddenly his hand shot forward and he grabbed the bird around its thick neck.

"Awk!" it squawked. "Your chains!"

"A friend of mine came along and snapped them for me," Prometheus smiled and his grip on the eagle's neck tightened. A huge man stepped from behind the rock. He had muscles that rippled like waves on the sea. "Meet Hercules. The greatest hero ever to walk the earth."

"Pleased to meet you, Herc!" the eagle gasped. "Er ... if you'll just let me go, Prom, I'll get off back to me nest."

"You're going nowhere," Prometheus promised.

"Nah! I was getting sick of liver anyway," the big bird said weakly.

"Hercules is going to kill you," Prometheus said calmly.

"Look Prommy ... mate ... old pal ... there was never anything personal, you know! I was only doing my job! Stone the crows, a bird's gotta do what a bird's gotta—"

His words were choked off with Prometheus's tight hand. He ignored the eagle's words. "But before I let Hercules kill you, guess what I'm going to do?"

"Er ... me liver?" the bird guessed.

Prometheus nodded.

"Aw, no, Prommy. It'll taste really nasty – yeuch! Honest! Really sour."

"Ah, but you're forgetting one thing, Eddie. There's nothing in this world that tastes so sweet as ... revenge!"

"DID YOU KNOW?
THE FOUNDERS OF ROME, ROMULUS AND REMUS, WERE SUPPOSED TO HAVE SURVIVED BEING LEFT TO DIE ON A HILLSIDE. A SHE-WOLF ADOPTED THEM. WHEN THEY GREW UP, ROMULUS KILLED REMUS AND CREATED ROME – NAMED AFTER ROMULUS, OF COURSE. IF HE HADN'T, THEN THIS BOOK MIGHT HAVE BEEN CALLED, THE ROTTEN REMANS!"

Rotten Roman Fun and Games

Rotten Roman games

Which of the following modern games do you think the Romans had?

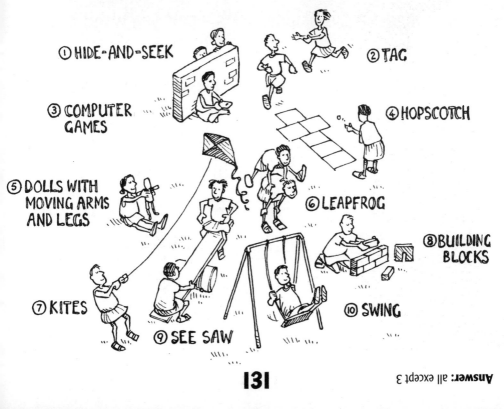

① HIDE-AND-SEEK

② TAG

③ COMPUTER GAMES

④ HOPSCOTCH

⑤ DOLLS WITH MOVING ARMS AND LEGS

⑥ LEAPFROG

⑦ KITES

⑧ BUILDING BLOCKS

⑨ SEE SAW

⑩ SWING

131

Some Roman games you might like to try

Roman children's games were a bit like ours ... only rottenly vicious at times!

Trigon

• Next time your parents slaughter a pig for dinner, ask them for the bladder – it's a part you won't be eating anyway.

• The bladder is cleaned out, then blown up like a balloon and tied.

OOPS

TIED TIGHT

THPURP

- A triangle with sides about two metres long is drawn on the ground and a player stands at each corner of the triangle.

- The bladder-ball is passed from one player to another without it touching the ground.

- The aim of the game is to keep the bladder-ball in the air as long as possible.

- Easy? Then add two more balls so that each player has one. There is no set order for passing the ball. You may have to pass your ball while receiving two from the other players! (Game hint: It helps to have three hands.)

- If you drop a ball you lose a point. The winner is the one with the fewest drops in the time – say five minutes. (If you can't find a dead pig then use tennis balls.)

Knucklebones

- If your parents happen to sacrifice a sheep to the gods, ask if you can have one of its feet.
- Boil the sheep's foot until the flesh and skin fall away from the bones.
- Take the small, cubic bones and dry them. You now have five "chuck stones".
- Hold the bones in one hand. Throw them into the air. The aim is to see who can catch the most on the back of the hand.

(Note: If your parents aren't sacrificing any sheep this week, you can use stones, dice or cubes of wood.)

GULP!

Micare

- Play in pairs.
- Each player places their right hand behind their back.
- Agree on a signal – one player will nod, for example.
- On the signal, both players shoot out the right hand with a number of fingers raised.
- At the same moment each player calls out what they guess the total number of fingers will be.
- If neither guesses correctly then try again.
- The winner is the first one to guess correctly. (Note: This sounds easy. In fact, the more you play it, the more you learn to use clever tactics. Try it and see.)

The Jar Game

- Someone is selected to be "It".
- "It" sits on the ground – they are said to be "in the jar". The others try to prod or nip the one on the ground – rotten Roman children could be pretty vicious while playing this. (Warning! Only pinch or punch "It" if "It" happens to be a teacher).
- The person in the jar cannot get up but they can try to grab hold of one of the touchers.
- The toucher who is grabbed goes into the jar.

Nuts

- Each player has a supply of nuts – probably hazel nuts.
- Each player adds a nut to her/his pile to build a pyramid.
- The winner is the player who uses the most nuts before the pyramid collapses.

(Note: This is a game for children. When you grew up the Romans would say you had "left your nuts". Perhaps you would like to ask your teacher, "When did you leave your nuts?")

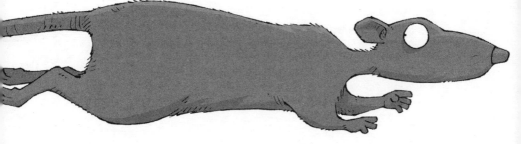

Blind Man's Buff

- Someone is chosen to be blindfolded.
- The other players each have a stick and dance around tapping the "blind man" with the stick, shouting "Come and catch me!", which the blindfolded person tries to do.
- If a player is caught then the blindfolded person tries to guess who s/he is holding.
- If the blindfolded person is right then the caught player becomes the blindfolded one.

FUNNY...
IT'S ALL
GONE
QUIET

Word games

If you like word games or crosswords then you might like to make a "square" of words. They should read the same whether they are read from left to right or from top to bottom.

Here's an example from Reading in Roman Britain (now in Berkshire) It was found scratched on a tile...

Sator means "a sower".

Arepo is a man's name.

Tenet means "he holds".

Opera means "work" or "deeds".

Rotas means "wheels".

The square has also been translated as "The sower, Arepo, guides the wheels carefully."

BUT ... some clever person worked out that this was not a word-game at all, but a secret, Christian prayer! Take all the letters and you can spell out the word PATERNOSTER. This is Latin for "Our Father" – the opening of the Lord's Prayer. There are two "A"s and two "O"s left over. These letters represent "the beginning and the end" to early Christians.

Clever, yes? But is it just coincidence? Or is it really a prayer? Make up your own mind.

Rotten grown-up games

The Romans enjoyed their circuses. But they weren't the sort of family day out we have at the circus today. No clowns, no jugglers, no tightrope walkers. But lots of violence, blood and death.

Augustine of Hippo wrote a book in which he told of his disgust at the bloodshed. His friend, Alypius, was taken to a Roman circus by some student friends. He set off for the circus, a real wimp. A band of trumpets played, bets were placed and the fighting began...

HE SHUT HIS EYES TIGHTLY, DETERMINED TO HAVE NOTHING TO DO WITH THESE HORRORS. IF ONLY HE HAD CLOSED HIS EARS AS WELL! THE FIGHT DREW A GREAT ROAR FROM THE CROWD! THIS THRILLED HIM SO DEEPLY THAT HE COULD NOT CONTAIN HIS CURIOSITY. WHEN HE SAW THE BLOOD IT WAS AS THOUGH HE HAD DRUNK A DEEP CUP OF SAVAGE PASSION. INSTEAD OF TURNING AWAY HE FIXED HIS EYES UPON THE SCENE AND DRANK IN ALL ITS FRENZY. HE REVELLED IN THE WICKEDNESS OF THE FIGHTING AND WAS DRUNK WITH THE FASCINATION OF THE BLOODSHED.

Julius Caesar, on the other hand, became a bit bored with the fighting and the dying. Long before the end of a contest he would begin reading reports and writing letters. This did not make him very popular with some of the spectators in the crowds!

Gruesome gladiators – ten terrible truths

1 The Romans brought the gladiator fights to Britain … battles between teams of armed men of whom half would be sure to lose their lives.

2 The idea of fighting and killing as a game probably began at funerals. The Roman Tertullian said...

ONCE UPON A TIME, PEOPLE BELIEVED THAT THE SOULS OF THE DEAD WERE KEPT HAPPY WITH HUMAN BLOOD, AND SO, AT FUNERALS, THEY SACRIFICED PRISONERS OF POOR QUALITY

DO I GET A SACRIFICE AT MY FUNERAL?

These sacrifices changed into fights to the death between two men at the funeral. They became so popular that they were taken away from the funeral and put in a huge arena. The fighters became known as gladiators.

3 In Rome there had been schools of gladiators. where a slave could train and fight for a gladiator master. If he won enough battles – and murdered enough opponents – he would win a fortune and his freedom. The greatest prize was the wooden sword a symbol of freedom.

4 Nutty Nero even ordered a battle between a woman and a dwarf as a special spectacle.

5 When a victim fell in a fight an attendant would smack him on the head with a hammer to make sure he was dead.

6 If a fighter gave up, exhausted, he could surrender. The emperor would then decide if he deserved to live or not. The crowd would usually tell him by screaming, "Mitte! Let him go!" or, "Iugula! Kill him!" The emperor would signal his decision with his thumb. Thumb down for death – thumb up for life. And we still use that sign today.

7 Some of the bloodiest battles were between criminals who were under sentence of death anyway. They fought till there was no one left – an unarmed man was put in the ring with an armed man who killed him. The armed man was then disarmed and the next man killed him. And so it went on – as soon as one victim fell, another was put in the ring.

8 There's not much evidence to show that the Romans in Britain brought the sort of wild animals to the arena that they brought to Rome itself.

9 There would be bears from Scotland, which were chained to a post and tormented for the entertainment of the crowd.

10 Back in Rome they would have seen…

• elephants fight against armed men – until one day, the elephants crashed through iron railings and trampled the crowd. Caesar had a moat built round the arena to protect the spectators from the animals.

• sea battles in an arena which could be flooded to take warships.

• animals fighting each other to the death – bear against buffalo, buffalo against elephant, elephant against rhinoceros.

• crocodiles, giraffes, hippopotami and ostriches – the crocodiles were tricky because they didn't survive very well when taken out of Africa. One lot spoiled the fun by refusing to eat!

• men against panthers, lions, leopards, tigers – but the men were usually heavily armed with spears, flaming torches, bows, lances and daggers. Some even took a pack of hounds into the arena to help them – they were in no more danger than the audience! One spectator made a joke about the emperor, Domitian. He was taken out of the crowd and thrown to a pack of dogs!

• men with cloaks against bulls – of the kind you can still see in Spain today.

• men fighting bears with their bare fists.

• five thousand beasts killed in one day of AD 80 in the Colosseum of Rome.

Amazing acts

But not every show in the arena was violent. Some of the acts used tame animals to perform tricks, rather as circus animals do today. The spectators were amused by...

- teams of tame panthers pulling chariots.
- a lion releasing a live hare from its mouth after it had caught it.
- a tiger licking the hand of its trainer.
- elephants kneeling in the sand in front of the emperor.
- elephants tracing Latin words in the sand with their trunks.

Petrifying plays

The Romans liked to visit the open-air theatres to watch plays. There were theatres in many of the bigger British towns. But if the plays were anything like the plays back in Rome, they would be banned today for being too violent!

The actors had real fights on stage. Then, Emperor Domitian allowed a real death on the stage. At the end of the play "Laureolis" the villain has to be crucified, tortured and torn apart by a bear. The actor playing the villain left the stage and his place was taken by a criminal who was under the sentence of death. The really rotten Romans enjoyed watching this horrible spectacle.

Then, of course, the Romans used the arenas as an excuse to execute people they didn't like – they put men, women and children in with wild animals, sometimes just for the simple crime of being Christians.

Strangely, it was the Christian religion that finally put an end to the massacres. When the emperors became Christian they banned the bloodthirsty events. On 1 October AD 326, Emperor Constantine put a stop to the gladiator schools and, by the end of the century, the shows had disappeared from the empire.

DID YOU KNOW?
THE TERM ROMAN HOLIDAY IS STILL USED TO DESCRIBE PEOPLE ENJOYING THEMSELVES BY WATCHING OTHERS SUFFERING. SO, WHEN TEACHERS TRY TO TELL YOU THE ROMANS "CIVILIZED" THE BARBARIANS, YOU CAN TELL THEM THAT THE ROTTEN ROMANS HAD SOME OF THE MOST "UNCIVILIZED FUN AND GAMES IN HISTORY."

Rotten Roman Food

The richest Romans enjoyed tasty foods and new recipes. They could afford spices to disguise the boring taste of the smoked or salted meat and fish.

Twenty foul food facts

1 The rich had great feasts. One Roman, called Trimalchio, held a feast which included wine that was a hundred years old. It also included a wild boar that, when sliced down the belly, allowed song-thrushes to fly out.

2 During such feasts some guests could eat so much that they had to be sick. They would then go back into the dining room to continue eating!

3 Emperor Maximian was a big eater. He was supposed to have eaten 20 kilograms of meat a day ... that's about all the meat you'd get from a small sheep!

4 Maximian also enjoyed about 34 litres of wine each day. Such gluttony killed him in the end, of course ... but not until he'd reigned almost 20 years!

5 In the kitchen, the rich kept a special container used for fattening up their dormice. They were fed on the very best food – walnuts, acorns and chestnuts, before being killed, stuffed and served as a great delicacy. The stuffing could be made from pork sausage (or even sausage made from other dormice) and flavoured with pepper and nuts.

6 Snails fattened in milk were popular. Take your live snails out of their shells and put them in a shallow dish of milk and salt for a day. They love milk so they slurp it down, but the salt just makes the stupid creatures thirstier! Then they are placed in plain milk for a few days. They drink and drink till they become too fat to get back in their shells. Fried in oil and served covered in wine sauce – they are delicious!

7 Even fouler … fatten up the snails on blood to add to their flavour. (Most snails would be vampire snails given the chance!)

8 The Romans enjoyed stuffed thrush. No worse than your Sunday chicken, right? Wrong! They stuffed the thrush through the throat without taking the insides out! Yeuch! The Romans also ate other birds that we wouldn't usually think of eating. They enjoyed…

- herring-gulls
- jackdaws
- peacocks
- ravens
- swans
- crows
- coots

9 The Romans didn't waste much. One recipe by Apicius calls for the chopped-up udder of a sow. They also ate the brains of animals … not to mention the lungs of goats and sheep.

10 King Mithradates of Pontus in Asia was scared of being poisoned, so he ate ... poison! In small doses, of course. That way his body built up a resistance to poison. Then he heard the Romans were coming to get him and he hadn't the guts to face them. So he swallowed poison. Of course, it didn't work! He had to fall on his sword in the end. (So, when the Romans found him he had even less guts!)

11 The Romans had some rotten sauces too. One was made from the guts of fish. They were salted and left to rot in the sun. After a few days the liquid was drained off and drunk or used as a sauce – the way you may sprinkle tomato ketchup on your chips. (This may sound a fishy story, but it's true!)

12 The Romans ate chicken, duck and goose, just as we still do. But the Romans probably served them at the table with the heads cut off but the feet still on!

13 In Roman times there were storks living in Britain. The Romans ate those too.

14 Horse bones have been found at Verulamium, which shows that the Romans ate horse-meat sausages. (Neigh! It's true!)

15 For vegetables, the Romans used some pretty odd things. Would you have eaten a salad made with dandelion leaves? How about an egg custard made with nettles? Or perhaps you'd prefer some stewed seaweed? These things are still eaten today in various parts of the world.

16 Sometimes, Roman banquet guests would drop rose petals into their wine.

17 At one meal, Heliogabalus served his guests 600 ostrich brains.

18 He also served peas mixed with grains of gold, and lentils mixed with precious stones – perhaps they liked rich food!

19 A favourite game was to disguise food so that it looked like something it wasn't! At one feast, roast piglets turned out to be made of pastry. At another, a nest seemed to be filled with eggs – but the eggs were made of pastry and inside, the "yolks" were made of spiced garden-warbler meat.

20 You might enjoy a meal while watching television. But could you eat at a Roman feast with dancers and acrobats, jugglers and clowns rushing around? Or even a pair of gladiators trying to kill each other?

The rotten Romans' daily diet

The main meals of the day for the Romans in Britain were:

MENU

BREAKFAST
BREAD AND FRUIT

LUNCH (PRANDIUM)
COLD EGGS, FISH OR VEGETABLES

DINNER (CENA)
GUSTATIO – TASTY THINGS LIKE RADISHES OR
ASPARAGUS AS A STARTER.
PRIMAE MENSALA – THE MAIN COURSE; CHICKEN OR
HARE AND FISH AND VEGETABLE DISHES.
SECUNDAE MENSAE – SWEET COURSE, INCLUDING
FRUIT

Rotten Roman beastly banquet

Why not invite your friends to a Roman-style banquet. Or, even better, invite your enemies.

First get your slaves to lay the table with napkins for each guest, a spoon and a knife. No forks, you will notice. If you want to try a Roman banquet then you'll have to eat with your fingers and have a napkin to keep your fingers clean! For the soft food and sauces you can use a spoon, and a knife for cutting or spearing meat.

Before you start, place some of your food in a small bowl in front of the statue of the family god. (If the god doesn't eat it then the slaves will!)

Say a few prayers. The Romans would say, "Auguste, patri patriae" – "Good luck to the emperor, father of our country."

Have your slaves wash and dry the feet of your guests. (If you can't find any slaves at the local supermarket or corner shop then you could always use a parent or teacher.)

Warning:
Do not cook this food yourself! Have it done for you by your slaves!

Starter (Gustatio)

If your local shop doesn't have stuffed dormice or snails fattened in milk, then you may like to try shellfish, hard-boiled eggs or a dish of olives. Serve with spiced wine – or in your case, grape juice!

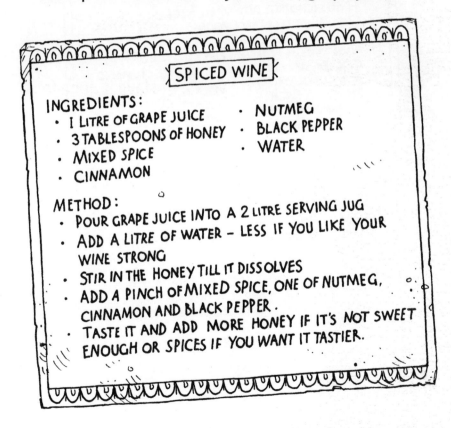

SPICED WINE

INGREDIENTS:
- 1 LITRE OF GRAPE JUICE
- 3 TABLESPOONS OF HONEY
- MIXED SPICE
- CINNAMON
- NUTMEG
- BLACK PEPPER
- WATER

METHOD:
- POUR GRAPE JUICE INTO A 2 LITRE SERVING JUG
- ADD A LITRE OF WATER – LESS IF YOU LIKE YOUR WINE STRONG
- STIR IN THE HONEY TILL IT DISSOLVES
- ADD A PINCH OF MIXED SPICE, ONE OF NUTMEG, CINNAMON AND BLACK PEPPER.
- TASTE IT AND ADD MORE HONEY IF IT'S NOT SWEET ENOUGH OR SPICES IF YOU WANT IT TASTIER.

Main Course (Primae Mensala)

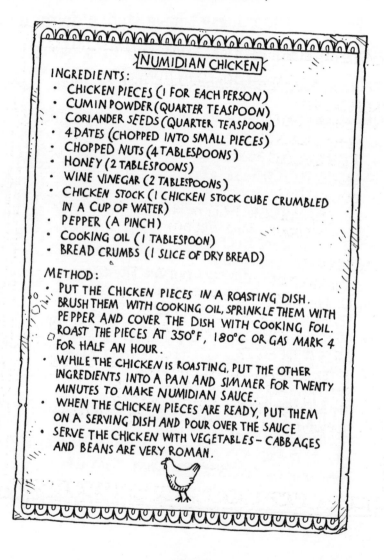

NUMIDIAN CHICKEN

INGREDIENTS:
- CHICKEN PIECES (1 FOR EACH PERSON)
- CUMIN POWDER (QUARTER TEASPOON)
- CORIANDER SEEDS (QUARTER TEASPOON)
- 4 DATES (CHOPPED INTO SMALL PIECES)
- CHOPPED NUTS (4 TABLESPOONS)
- HONEY (2 TABLESPOONS)
- WINE VINEGAR (2 TABLESPOONS)
- CHICKEN STOCK (1 CHICKEN STOCK CUBE CRUMBLED IN A CUP OF WATER)
- PEPPER (A PINCH)
- COOKING OIL (1 TABLESPOON)
- BREAD CRUMBS (1 SLICE OF DRY BREAD)

METHOD:
- PUT THE CHICKEN PIECES IN A ROASTING DISH. BRUSH THEM WITH COOKING OIL, SPRINKLE THEM WITH PEPPER AND COVER THE DISH WITH COOKING FOIL. ROAST THE PIECES AT 350°F, 180°C OR GAS MARK 4 FOR HALF AN HOUR.
- WHILE THE CHICKEN IS ROASTING, PUT THE OTHER INGREDIENTS INTO A PAN AND SIMMER FOR TWENTY MINUTES TO MAKE NUMIDIAN SAUCE.
- WHEN THE CHICKEN PIECES ARE READY, PUT THEM ON A SERVING DISH AND POUR OVER THE SAUCE
- SERVE THE CHICKEN WITH VEGETABLES – CABBAGES AND BEANS ARE VERY ROMAN.

Sweet Course (Secundae Mensae)

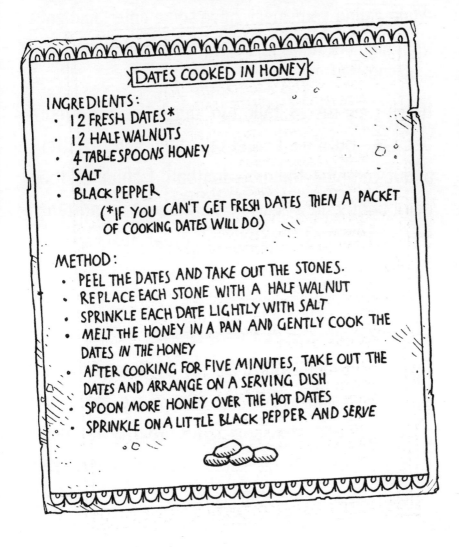

DATES COOKED IN HONEY

INGREDIENTS:
- 12 FRESH DATES*
- 12 HALF WALNUTS
- 4 TABLESPOONS HONEY
- SALT
- BLACK PEPPER
  (*IF YOU CAN'T GET FRESH DATES THEN A PACKET OF COOKING DATES WILL DO)

METHOD:
- PEEL THE DATES AND TAKE OUT THE STONES.
- REPLACE EACH STONE WITH A HALF WALNUT
- SPRINKLE EACH DATE LIGHTLY WITH SALT
- MELT THE HONEY IN A PAN AND GENTLY COOK THE DATES IN THE HONEY
- AFTER COOKING FOR FIVE MINUTES, TAKE OUT THE DATES AND ARRANGE ON A SERVING DISH
- SPOON MORE HONEY OVER THE HOT DATES
- SPRINKLE ON A LITTLE BLACK PEPPER AND SERVE

Finish off with fruit and nuts and grape-juice wine. While eating your meal, have some entertainment from jugglers, dancers, singers or musicians.

It isn't polite to talk too much at a Roman banquet. But if you must talk, then don't chatter about common things – football, fashion or the neighbour's new car – talk about important things like life, death and great teachers of our time.

Rotten Roman remedies

It didn't do to be sick in Roman times. Sometimes the cure was worse than the illness! Here's a letter from a Roman, Cassius, to his sister, Juliet. Would you like to try some of his cures…?

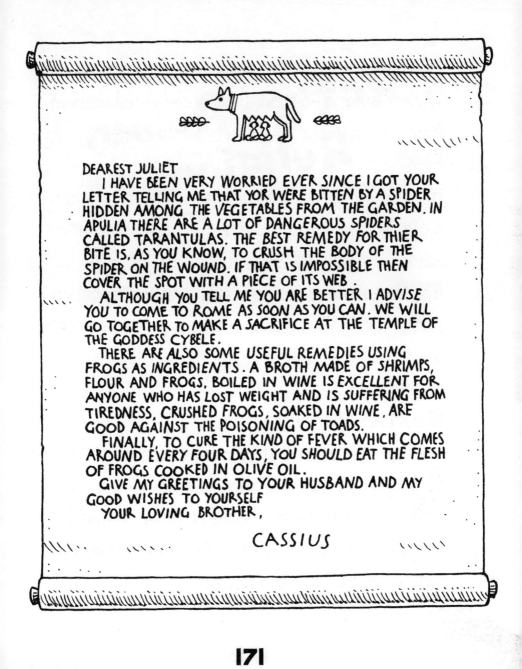

DEAREST JULIET
I HAVE BEEN VERY WORRIED EVER SINCE I GOT YOUR
LETTER TELLING ME THAT YOR WERE BITTEN BY A SPIDER
HIDDEN AMONG THE VEGETABLES FROM THE GARDEN. IN
APULIA THERE ARE A LOT OF DANGEROUS SPIDERS
CALLED TARANTULAS. THE BEST REMEDY FOR THIER
BITE IS, AS YOU KNOW, TO CRUSH THE BODY OF THE
SPIDER ON THE WOUND. IF THAT IS IMPOSSIBLE THEN
COVER THE SPOT WITH A PIECE OF ITS WEB.
    ALTHOUGH YOU TELL ME YOU ARE BETTER I ADVISE
YOU TO COME TO ROME AS SOON AS YOU CAN. WE WILL
GO TOGETHER TO MAKE A SACRIFICE AT THE TEMPLE OF
THE GODDESS CYBELE.
    THERE ARE ALSO SOME USEFUL REMEDIES USING
FROGS AS INGREDIENTS. A BROTH MADE OF SHRIMPS,
FLOUR AND FROGS, BOILED IN WINE IS EXCELLENT FOR
ANYONE WHO HAS LOST WEIGHT AND IS SUFFERING FROM
TIREDNESS. CRUSHED FROGS, SOAKED IN WINE, ARE
GOOD AGAINST THE POISONING OF TOADS.
    FINALLY, TO CURE THE KIND OF FEVER WHICH COMES
AROUND EVERY FOUR DAYS, YOU SHOULD EAT THE FLESH
OF FROGS COOKED IN OLIVE OIL.
    GIVE MY GREETINGS TO YOUR HUSBAND AND MY
GOOD WISHES TO YOURSELF
    YOUR LOVING BROTHER,

            CASSIUS

171

Rotten Roman Religions

The Romans brought their religion and their gods with them from Rome, though in time they became mixed with the native British religions.

Lucky charms and cruel curses

In the Roman home the Lares were very important. These were household gods. They protected the home from evil spirits. In richer homes, Romans would also worship gods like...

Vesta – goddess of the fire and hearth ... and you can still buy matches called "Vestas"!

Penates – guardian of the store cupboard ... made sure nobody sneaked any midnight feasts.

Janus – the two-faced god who used his two faces to watch the people coming into the house and those going out.

The hot spring waters in the city of Bath are used as cures for all sorts of illnesses by people today. They were used by the Romans too. The Romans were a bit superstitious and believed there was magic in the water. They threw things into the water to take advantage of its powers. They threw coins in probably as you would into a wishing well – 12,000 Roman coins have been found there.

They also threw in written tablets, usually trying to make a deal with a god – "You do this for me, god, and I'll build an altar for you, OK?"

Many of these requests were for curses – if the name of the person you wanted to curse was written backwards, then the magic would be even stronger.

One man lost his girlfriend, Vilbia, to another man. He scratched the curse on a piece of metal … but wrote it backwards. Then he threw it in the water where it was found hundreds of years later. It read…

> RETAW EKIL DIUQIL OTNI NRUT OT EM MORF
> AIBLIV KOOT OHW NOSREP EHT TNAW I

(Do you know anyone you'd like to turn into a real drip?)

An even nastier curse has been found in Clothall. It was nailed onto some object, perhaps a dead animal, and says …

> TACITA IS CURSED BV THIS AND WILL
> BE DECAYED LIKE ROTTING BLOOD.

The rottenest Roman religions

Chucking chickens

The Roman army had its own religions and its own superstitions. The General of an army would look at the liver of certain animals for signs as to how a battle might go. They might also...

• observe the flight of birds – the ways in which crows flew, for example.

• observe the way the sacred chickens ate their food – Claudius Pulcher took chickens with him on a voyage to the Punic wars. The chickens were probably a bit seasick, because they refused to eat at all – a bad sign. So Claudius Pulcher ordered them to be thrown overboard with the words, "If they won't eat then let them drink!" He went on to lose the battle and the soldiers blamed him for drowning the sacred chickens!

Stomach signals

A Roman teacher, Fronto, wrote to his pupil, Marcus, with news that he had a pain in the stomach. He believed this was a sign from the gods that there was bad luck coming to his family. (If your teacher had a pain in the stomach, she'd be more likely to blame school dinners!)

Mighty Mithras

The religion of the bull-god Mithras, was very popular with many Roman soldiers. He was probably brought to Britain by the legionaries who served in Persia, where Mithras was a popular god.

Mithras was the "judge" of the afterlife – he decided who should go to heaven and who should go to hell after they died.

The temples of Mithras were dark and gloomy places – sometimes underground – and a lot of the soldiers must have enjoyed joining this religion, because it was like joining a secret society.

You couldn't enter the temples until you'd performed certain brave deeds – like allowing yourself to be locked up for several hours in a coffin! The base of the coffin was on the stone-cold floor and the side was close to a fire – you froze and fried at the same time!

Bull's blood

Another Eastern "mystery" religion had equally gruesome rituals, as Prudentius described in the 4th century AD...

66 THE WORSHIPPERS DIG A DEEP PIT AND THE HIGH PRIEST IS LOWERED INTO IT. ABOVE HIM THEY PUT A PLATFORM OF LOOSE PLANKS. EACH PLANK HAS TINY HOLES DRILLED IN IT. A HUGE BULL IS STOOD ON THE PLATFORM. THEY TAKE A SACRED HUNTING SPEAR AND DRIVE IT INTO THE BULL'S

HEART. THE HOT BLOOD SPURTS OUT OF THE DEEP WOUND. IT FALLS THROUGH THE HOLES IN THE PLANKS LIKE ROTTEN RAIN ONTO THE PRIEST BELOW. HIS CLOTHES AND BODY ARE COVERED IN THE ANIMAL'S GORE. AFTERWARDS HE CLIMBS OUT OF THE PIT. IT IS A DREADFUL SIGHT TO SEE. "

Christianity

From the end of the first century AD, Christianity began to enter Britain. After the exciting Roman religions some Christians seemed a bit boring. One Christian writer, Tertullian, was against fancy clothes – he didn't even like to see them dyed.

He wrote...

IF GOD HAD WANTED US TO WEAR PURPLE AND SKY-BLUE CLOTHES, THEN HE WOULD HAVE GIVEN US PURPLE AND SKY-BLUE SHEEP!

By AD **250**, the emperors began stamping out Christianity and killing Christians. St Alban was one of the victims in Britain. Still, Christianity continued to grow there.

Then, in AD **313**, the Act of Toleration was passed that allowed Christians to worship openly. But it was all too late for poor old Alban...

PURPLE? WITH ALL THAT GREEN GRASS AROUND? WE'D CLASH!

The legend of St Alban

The wind blew wild and wet along the wall. Two soldiers shivered behind their shields and complained.

"End of the world, this place. End of the world!" old Laganus groaned.

"Not quite the end of the world," his young partner pointed out. "There are people on the other side of the wall"

"People!" Laganus laughed. "Them Picts aren't *people.*' More what you'd call *animals.* Proper people wouldn't live out in that wild country. They're *savages*, Paul, *savages.*"

Young Paul huddled into his cloak and looked across the bleak and empty moors. "Not as savage as the Romans can be," he said carefully.

"That's no way to talk about our masters!"

Laganus gasped. "That's the sort of talk that'll get you beaten!"

Paul nodded. "That's what I mean. They'll beat me. They're cruel."

The older man snorted. "You're just soft, my boy. You've got to kill your enemy. Kill or get yourself killed. That's the way it is!"

"You wouldn't say that if you were a Christian," Paul told him.

Laganus turned on him savagely. "Yeh! I've heard all about your Christian God! Look at that Alban!"

"They killed him! Paul cried. "The Romans killed him!"

"But that's nothing to what your kind and gentle God did for revenge, is it?" the old soldier sneered.

He sat down in the shelter of the wall and rubbed his freezing hands. "I heard the true story from a soldier of the Seventh Legion last week."

Paul crouched down beside him. Alban was a hero. A Christian martyr…"

"Alban was a soldier just like you or me. Well, more like you, Paul. He was soft-hearted. Soft in the head too, if you ask me. The Romans were having one of their crackdowns on the Christians. You know the sort of thing. Killing a few here and there to show them who is boss."

"Murder," Paul muttered.

"Alban was a *Roman* soldier, of course. He should have been joining in the *killing* of the Christians. Instead he gave *shelter* to a Christian priest."

"Amphibalus," the young soldier nodded.

"And worse! He let this Amphibalus talk *him* into becoming a Christian!" Laganus groaned. "They sent soldiers to arrest Alban, of course. What did he do? Disguised himself and tried to run away."

"They caught him," Paul sighed.

"Of course they caught him! But they didn't kill him for hiding the enemy – they didn't kill him for becoming a Christian..."

"They did!" Paul cut in.

"No, no, no! They gave him a chance. They told him to make a sacrifice to the Roman gods. Prove that he was still loyal!" the old soldier said.

"He refused."

"So it serves him right if he was sentenced to death," Laganus snorted. "But the Romans didn't have him tortured or crucified or stoned to death. No. They were kind. They sentenced him to a quick death by beheading!"

"They murdered him," Paul repeated stubbornly.

"Ah, but that was quick and kind. What happened at the execution, eh? You Christians never tell about that!"

The young soldier shrugged. "I don't know."

Laganus grinned. Two soldiers led Alban to the place of execution. Alban managed to convert one of them on the way. But he didn't convert the second one, did he? The second executioner cut off Alban's head! *Then* your 'kind', kind God took his cruel, cruel revenge. As Alban's head hit the ground the executioner staggered back clutching his face. When the guards reached him they found that his eyes had both dropped out! Plop! Plop!"

By the end of that century, Christianity became the religion of the Roman State. But some parts of the British Isles were converted as the result of a strange accident…

Pirates, pagans and Patrick

Did you know?

I Patrick is the patron saint of Ireland, BUT he was born in Wales, lived in England and his parents were Roman.

2 When he was 16 he was kidnapped by Celtic pirates and taken as a slave to Ireland.

3 He was given a rotten job by the Irish pagans. Looking after cattle on the bleak hills.

4 A boulder crashed down the mountainside towards Patrick. Just before it flattened him it split in two. One piece went on either side of him.

5 Patrick took this as a miracle. He believed it was a sign from God that there was special work for him.

6 He escaped to Gaul, then returned home to become a farmer. He still felt that his life had been saved for some special reason.

7 He boldly went back to Ireland.

8 He performed miracles there. There is a story, for example, that there are no snakes in Ireland because Patrick got rid of them all.

9 Patrick converted the kings of many Irish kingdoms to Christianity. The kings were baptised and the people followed the kings.

10 A king of southern Ireland had a rotten baptism. Patrick carried a crook – like a shepherd. It was pointed on the bottom. During the baptism Patrick accidentally put the point clean through the king's foot. The king didn't complain; he thought it was all part of the ceremony.

Rotten Roman Facts

The rottenest Roman historian

At the eastern end of the Roman Wall is a fort. In 1971 the museum at the fort proudly showed their latest find. "It is a sestertius coin, made between AD 135 and AD 138. On the back of the coin is a large letter 'R' – standing for Roma," they said.

Then an expert, Miss Fiona Gordon, told them they were wrong. The sestertius was, in fact, a free gift given away with bottles of fruit squash. "The letter 'R' stands for the name of the makers, Robinson!"

The museum keepers discovered Miss Gordon was correct. That was embarrassing! But, most embarrassing of all, Miss Fiona Gordon was just nine years old!

True or false?

1 A favourite method of execution in ancient Rome was "stinging to death".

2 The Roman Fort at Sinodum is supposed to be the site of a money-pit full of buried treasure.

3 Druids picked their victims by going "Eeny-meeny-miney-mo..."

REMIND ME, WHAT COMES AFTER MO?

4 Women could be Druids.

5 Druids would stab a victim in the back, then see the future from the way he died.

6 A crash at a chariot race was called "a plane-crash".

7 The Victorians pulled down the east end of Hadrian's Wall and used the stone to mend their roads.

8 The Romans didn't have peppermint toothpaste. They preferred powdered mouse-brains.

9 The Romans stopped traffic jams in Aldborough by building a bypass.

10 In Roman horse races the losing horse was killed.

Answers

1 True – the victim was smothered in honey then covered with angry wasps.

2 True – in the 19th century a local villager was digging at the fort one day when he came across an iron chest. A raven landed on it and said, "He is not born yet!" The villager thought this meant, "The person who can open the chest is not yet born." He filled the hole in and left. Are you the one born to open the chest?

3 True – according to Victorian experts. The shepherds of ancient Britain would count sheep with a number system that sounded very like "Eeny-meeny-miney-mo". The Druids could well have used it. Children may then have copied it as part of a gruesome game and it's been used in children's games ever since.

4 True – the Romans said that they met Druidesses. These women were good at telling fortunes.

5 True – the Roman historian, Strabo, said the way a man twisted and fell after he had been stabbed helped a Druid to read the fortunes for his tribe.

6 False – it was called a "shipwreck".

7 True. There are still large stretches of Hadrian's wall to be seen across the north of England. It's well looked after now ... but it hasn't always been. Farmers pinched stones from the Wall to build their houses, and the Victorians were worse. They pulled the wall down, smashed up the stones into little bits and used them to repair the roads of Newcastle!

8 True – perhaps they wanted their teeth to be "squeaky" clean! They also used powdered horn, oyster-shell ash and the ashes of dogs' teeth mixed with honey.

9 True.

10 False – the winning horse was killed as a sacrifice to the god of war, Mars. The local people often fought fiercely to decide who would have the honour of sticking its head on their wall.

Rotten Roman towns

Everyone tells you about how marvellous the Roman baths were. But not all of the Romans were so keen. One Roman wrote…

I LIVE ABOVE THE PUBLIC BATHS, AND WE ALL KNOW WHAT THAT MEANS. YEUCH! IT'S SICKENING FIRSTLY THERE ARE THE STRONG MEN DOING EXERCISES, SWINGING LEAD WEIGHTS ROUND WITH GRUNTS AND GROANS. THEN THERE ARE THE LAZY ONES HAVING A CHEAP MASSAGE — I CAN HEAR THEM BEING SLAPPED ON THE BACK. THEN THERE ARE THE NOISES OF FIGHTERS AND THIEVES BEING ARRESTED. WORST IS THE SOUND OF THE MAN WHO LIKES TO HEAR HIS OWN VOICE IN THE BATH. AND WHAT ABOUT THE ONES WHO LEAP INTO THE BATH AND MAKE A HUGE SPLASH IN THE WATER?

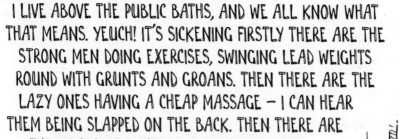

SPLASH

LA LA LA

SLAP

LA LA

CHATTER CHATTER

GROAN

ONE TWO ONE TWO

SLAP SLAP

GRUNT

OW!

Rotten Romans today

The rotten Romans ran the world for a long time. There are still signs of their life today.

Did you know?

1 The Romans signed their "trademark" wherever they went. They wrote the letters SPQR, which stood for Senatus Populus Que Romanus — The Senate and the People of Rome. The buses and the drain covers of Rome have the letters on them today.

2 The Roman language is called Latin. It is still used in some religious ceremonies and used to be taught in many schools. But no one speaks it as an everyday language now. So it's called a "dead" language. That's why schoolchildren who still have to learn it mutter the same old school chant...

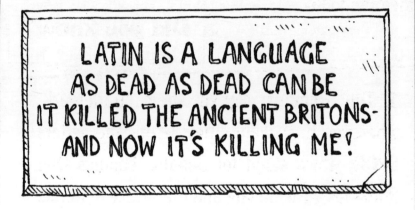

LATIN IS A LANGUAGE
AS DEAD AS DEAD CAN BE
IT KILLED THE ANCIENT BRITONS-
AND NOW IT'S KILLING ME!

3 Much of the Roman Wall can still be seen – and walked along – in the north of England. But the famous historian and monk, St Bede, got his facts about Hadrian's wall completely wrong! He said the Romans built it just before they abandoned Britain. It was a sort of farewell present for the Britons, planned to keep the Picts and Scots out. He wrote...

"WHEN THE WALL WAS FINISHED, THE ROMANS GAVE CLEAR ADVICE TO THE DEJECTED BRITONS, THEN SAID GOODBYE TO THEIR FRIENDS AND NEVER RETURNED. THE GLOOMY BRITISH SOLDIERS LIVED IN TERROR DAY AND NIGHT. BEYOND THE WALL THE ENEMY CONSTANTLY ATTACKED THEM WITH HOOKED WEAPONS, DRAGGING THE DEFENDERS DOWN FROM THE WALL AND DASHING THEM TO THE GROUND. AT LAST THE BRITONS ABANDONED THEIR CITIES AND THE WALL AND FLED IN CONFUSION."

Wrong! The Wall was there 300 years before the Romans left. Don't believe everything you read in history books – even if the writer is a saint!

4 There are some rotten things in Britain today that we can blame the Romans for. They brought them here. Things like…

• stinging nettles – next time you sit on one, you can cry out in agony, "Oooh! The rotten Romans!"

• cabbages and peas – the sort of vegetables your parents make you eat because "they're good for you." Next time you hear that, you can say, "The ancient Britons survived a few million years without them!"

• cats – yes, blame the Romans for that mangy moggy that yowls all night on the corner of your street and keeps you awake. When teacher tells you off for yawning in class, say, "Don't blame me – blame the rotten Romans!"

5 Rotten spelling – a lot of the words we use today come from Latin. They made sense to the rotten Romans but they don't make sense to us. Take the Latin word "plumbum"... no, it doesn't mean purple bottom. It means waterworks. So we get a word for a man who fixes your leaky waterworks from that. That's right, "plumber". We say it "plummer" and any sensible Briton in their right mind would spell it "plummer". But the Romans put that useless "b" in the middle, so we have to. Next time you get two out of ten for your spelling test say, "Don't blame me – blame the rotten Romans!"

6 False teeth – the Romans generally had good teeth. They cleaned them regularly and didn't have sugar to rot them. But, if they did lose a tooth, they used false teeth. These would be made of gold or ivory. They'd be held in place with gold wire. That wire could also be used to hold loose teeth in place. The poor people just had to let them drop out.

Ancient Roman ancient joke:

DOCTOR DOCTOR! HAVE YOU GOT SOMETHING TO KEEP MY TEETH IN?

CERTAINLY, MADAM, HERE'S A PAPER BAG!

7 Skyscrapers – the Romans made buildings with more floors than anyone else of their age. But this led to some rotten Roman tragedies. In 217 BC an ox escaped from the local market. It ran into a three-storey building and up the stairs. When it reached the top it threw itself out of a window on the top floor. By the time of Augustus the crowded cities were forcing people to build houses higher and higher – a bit like Britain in the 1960s! But many of these tower blocks began to collapse – so Augustus passed a law banning any building over 20 metres tall.

8 A family living in Hertford, England, are so keen on the Romans that they eat Roman food (like sardines stuffed with dates – yeuch!) and play Roman games after dinner. The family have organized a new Fourteenth Legion (but with only 24 legionaries so far) who go on 40-kilometre marches just as the original legion did. They also dress as Romans occasionally and go around schools to give demonstrations to children. This does not always have the desired result – sometimes younger pupils see the Roman soldier walk into the classroom and they burst into tears … usually the boys! Oh, and the daughter of the family isn't a fan of the Romans and is too embarrassed by her Roman family to bring her boyfriend home!

9 We have Christmas traditions today that live on from Roman times. One tradition is Roman and one British. They were…

- holly – the Romans had ceremonies for their god, Saturn in December. The decoration they used was holly. Country people still believe that it's a protection against poison, storms, fire and "the evil eye".

- mistletoe – trees were sacred to the Britons. Mistletoe grew on trees and sucked the spirit from them – that's the sticky juice in the berries. The oak was the most sacred tree, so mistletoe from the oak was the most precious plant of all. Druids in white robes cut it with golden knives on the sixth day of a new moon. A sprig over the door protected the house from thunder, lightning and all evil.

10 Christianity put an end to the Druids' human sacrifices … but 2,000 years later we may still have curious memories of those deadly days … the children's game London Bridge is Falling Down. Some form of this game is known all over the world.

Two children link hands and form an arch. The rest of the children have to pass under the arch while chanting the song. When a child is caught, then the bridge has fallen. That child becomes the "watchman" of the bridge.

But the legends say that, in the days of pagan beliefs, the unlucky child could only guard the bridge if he (or she) was dead! It seems the spirits of rivers hate bridges and without a sacrifice they would bring it down. The British legend says that children were sacrificed and their blood poured over the stones of the first London Bridge to keep "Old Father Thames" happy.

Epilogue

The Romans left to defend their homeland and Rome. The Britons were left to defend the island against enemies old and new. A historian from those times, Gildas, described how the "foul" Picts and Scots with their "lust for blood" swarmed over Hadrian's mighty Wall. They pulled the British defenders down from the Wall and killed them like "lambs are slaughtered by butchers". The men from the north with their hairy "hang-dog" faces took over.

Four hundred years before, the Britons had fought the Romans off. But in four hundred years the Britons had forgotten how to fight. Suddenly the Romans didn't seem so rotten after all. Now the Britons wrote and begged them to return…

> **"THE BARBARIANS DRIVE US TO THE SEA, THE SEA DRIVES US BACK TO THE BARBARIANS. BETWEEN THESE TWO METHODS OF DEATH WE ARE EITHER MASSACRED OR DROWNED."**

But no help came. Rome had problems of its own. After hundreds of years of Roman rule, Britain entered "The Dark Ages".

ROTTEN ROMANS

Quiz

Evil emperors

It's really weird but true. Some of the battiest people in history have been leaders – kings and queens, emperors and empresses, presidents and princes. It's almost as if you have to be slightly potty to be a ruler!

Rome had their fair share of rotten rulers. Here are a few foul facts about them. Only the odd word has been left out for you to complete...

Here are the missing words, in the wrong order: mother, head, chicken, horse, corpse, cobweb, cheese, wife, wrinkly, leg.

1 Augustus Caesar (31 BC–AD 14) caught Brutus, the murderer of Julius Caesar, and had his _____ thrown at the feet of Caesar's statue.

2 Tiberius (AD 14–37) said that he would smash the
_____ of anyone who disobeyed him.

3 Caligula (AD 37–41) wanted someone to help him
to rule so he gave the job to his _____.

4 Claudius (AD 41–54) had his _____ executed.

5 Nero (AD 54–68) tried to drown his _____.

6 Vitellius (AD 69) had his _____ thrown in the
River Tiber at Rome.

7 Hadrian (AD 117–138) forced a _____ to commit
suicide.

8 Antonius (AD 138–161) died of eating too much
_____.

9 Eliogabalus (AD 218–222) had the curious hobby
of collecting every _____ he could find.

10 Honorius (AD 395–423) had a _____ called
'Rome'.

Stabbing Jules

Julius Caesar was a brilliant Roman leader, but he
became a bit too big for his boots – his red boots,
in fact. The Romans were now used to having
leaders who were "elected". They had hated their
old kings ... who had worn red boots instead of a
crown, but when the booted-up kings were kicked

out the Romans got on much better with their elected leaders.

But Julius got himself elected for life. Just like a king. When he started wearing red boots, his number was up. There was just one way to get rid of him then – assassination.

His friend Brutus led the murderers, who struck when Caesar was entering the Roman parliament (the senate). Roman writer Plutarch told the gory story. Can you sort out the scrambled words in this version?

Some of Brutus's gang slipped behind Caesar's chair while others came to meet him. Cimber grabbed Caesar's robe and pulled it from his neck. This was the A SLING for the attack.

Casca struck the first blow. His IF KEN

made a wound in ASS ACRE neck but Caesar was able to turn round, grab the knife and hold on. The HAT CREWS were horrified but didn't dare move or make a sound.

Each AS SINS AS bared his dagger now. They pushed Caesar this way and that like a wild BE SAT surrounded by hunters.

Brutus stabbed Caesar in the groin. Above all Caesar had RED TUTS Brutus. When he saw Brutus coming towards him he pulled his robe over his head and sank down.

The attackers pushed Caesar against the ASTUTE of his old enemy Pompey. The statue became drenched with DO LOB.

Caesar received 23 wounds. Many of the assassins WON DUDE each other as they fought to stick so many knives into one body.

Foul Roman food

Do you know what the rotten Romans ate? Have a go at this quirky quiz on cuisine (that's a posh word for "cooking") and find out…

1 The Romans didn't have tomato ketchup but they did have sauce made from what?

a sheep eyeballs

b fish guts

c elephant's tail

MY HAMBURGER IS BLINKING!

2 At posh Roman feasts guests sometimes ate more than their stomachs could hold. How?

a They emptied their stomachs by vomiting every now and then.

b They stretched their stomachs with special exercises.

c They stuck a pin in their stomach to let out trapped air and let in more food.

3 Snails were fattened up before they were killed. They were kept in a bowl of what?

a chopped cabbage

b brains

c blood

4 Emperor Eliogabalus also served a meal where the peas were mixed with what?

a queues

b poison

c gold nuggets

5 Emperor Eliogabalus served 600 of them at one feast. What?

a ostrich brains

b ducks' feet

c camel-burgers

6 A Roman called Trimalchio had a feast with a roasted boar. When it was sliced down the belly, what came out?

a maggots

b songbirds

c a dancing girl

7 What could you watch as you ate at some Roman feasts?

a television

b two gladiators trying to murder one another

c tap-dancing bears

TICKETTY
TICKETTY
TICKETTY

TICKETTY
TICKETTY
TICKETTY

8 The Romans ate cute little pets that you probably wouldn't eat. What?

a cats

b budgies

c dormice

9 The Romans did not eat animals' what?

a teeth

b brains

c lungs

10 Emperor Maximian was a strange eater. Why?

a He was the only vegetarian emperor.

b He ate only eggs and drank only water.

c He ate 20 kilos of meat a day.

Answers

Evil emperors

1 head. Nice present for Jules!

2 leg. Tiberius died at the age of 78, probably suffocated by his chief helper.

3 horse. Cruel Caligula liked to feed criminals to wild animals. He was stabbed to death by one of his guards.

4 wife. She was a bit of a flirt. But he also had 300 of her party friends chopped too! His third wife, and niece, had him poisoned with mushrooms.

5 mother. When the plot failed he sent soldiers to give her the chop. Nero stabbed himself to death before his enemies got to him.

6 corpse. He was murdered in the centre of Rome but not given a nice emperor's burial.

7 wrinkly. Hadrian accused Servianus of treason and forced him to kill himself. But Servianus was 90 years old and hardly a big threat.

8 cheese. At least that's what a Roman historian blamed his death on. Guess it was just hard cheese.

9 cobweb. Maybe he was planning to build the world's first web-site?

10 chicken. Trouble is he loved the chicken Rome more than he loved the city Rome, and the city was neglected.

Stabbing Jules

These are the unscrambled words in the correct order: signal; knife; Caesar's; watchers; assassin; beast; trusted; statue; blood; wounded.

Foul Roman food

1b The guts were soaked in salt water and left to stew in the sun for a few days. Then the fish-gut sauce was poured over the food as a tasty treat. Oh my cod!

2a They used a stick with a feather to tickle their tonsils and vomited into a bowl. When their stomach was empty they went back and ate more. Scoff-vomit, scoff-vomit, scoff-vomit all night long.

3c The snails supped the blood till they were too fat to get in their shells. The blood diet made them taste nice. If they wanted creamy snails, the Romans fed them on milk before eating them.

4c Eliogabalus mixed gold and precious stones with the peas as a sort of treat. But if one of those diamonds smashed your teeth you'd be sore. And if you swallowed a gold nugget you'd be ill! You'd have to sit on the toilet and wait for some change!

5a Ostrich brains are quite small so he'd need 600 to keep his guests fed. But where did he get all those ostriches? Zoo knows?

6b There were thrushes stuffed inside the roast boar. (Were they bored in there?) Trimalchio also served wine that was 100 years old at that feast.

7b Of course, the trouble with gladiators fighting as you eat is that they could splash blood and guts all over your freshly cooked dinner. Aren't you lucky you don't suffer that while you watch telly?

8c They fed the dormice really well on walnuts, acorns and chestnuts. They were served roasted and stuffed with pork sausage. Scrummy! Even tastier than hamster or gerbil!

9a They ate all sorts of other things though. As well as sheep and goat lungs or brains, they ate gulls, peacocks, swans and jackdaws. They stuffed the birds just by pushing stuffing straight down their throats. They didn't clean the insides out the way you do with your Christmas turkey. Yeuch!

10c That's about a small sheep every day. Would ewe believe it? He was also supposed to have drunk about 34 litres of wine ... but it must have been very weak. Of course, after 20 years all that eating killed him, but he was probably too drunk to notice he was dead!

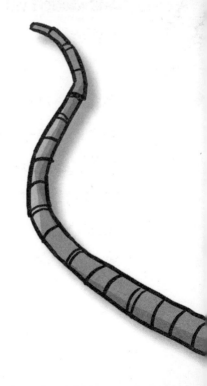

Interesting Index

Britain 12, 14, 16, 71–2, 101, 178, 182–3, 189, 196, 202–3, 206, 210
    Celts in 53, 59–60
    childhood in 115
    food in 164
    fun in 139, 143, 147, 152
    religion in 172
Britannicus (Nero's brother) 93–4
Britons 25, 55–6, 63–4, 201–3, 211
Brutus (Roman senator) 78–80, 82, 102, 214, 217–18
burial sites 73–4, 106–7

calendar 102
Caligula (Roman emperor) 88–91, 101, 215, 224
Caracalla (Roman emperor) 105–6
Caractacus (son of Cunobelinus) 63–72
Carthage (North African city) 10–11
Cartimandua (queen of Brigantes) 68–9, 72, 110
Catuvellauni (British tribe) 63
Celts (European tribes) 37–62, 110, 189

Centurions 20
charms, lucky 116–17, 172–5
chickens 103, 214, 226
    Numidian 168
    sacred 176–7
    seasick 176
children 108–19
Christians 14, 152, 182–91, 209
    persecuted 95
    secret prayer of 140
Claudius (Roman emperor) 12 69, 71–2, 92, 95, 215
cobwebs, collecting 102, 226
Colosseum (cruel circus) 149
Constantine (Roman emperor) 14, 153
criminals
    as animal feed 89, 224
    battling 147
    torn apart 152
    tortured 92, 152
crucifixion 62, 95, 152, 187
curses 172, 174–5
Cybele (goddess) 171

Dark Ages 212
doctors, dreadful 22, 35–6
dogs
    teeth 197
    thrown to 149

NEW FOR 2013

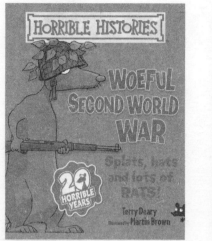

Horrible Histories:
Filling children's heads with foul facts since 1993